Interview
With A
SPY

Revelations on the
John F. Kennedy
Assassination and the
Impact on My Generation
of Young Americans

INTERVIEW WITH A SPY
REVELATIONS ON THE JOHN F. KENNEDY ASSASSINATION
AND THE IMPACT ON MY GENERATION OF YOUNG AMERICANS

First edition. May 2025.

Published by Big Kat Kreative LLC, 2025.
Printed in the United States of America.

Cover designed by Amy Ferrante

ISBN: 978-1-962796-10-1

Written by Kevin F. Jursinski

Interview With A SPY

Revelations on the
John F. Kennedy
Assassination and the
Impact on My Generation
of Young Americans

Kevin F. Jursinski

To my incredible wife Darlene
and our daughters, Jamie, Lauren and Kara.
These amazing women are my foundation.
Thanks for all your love and support.

To my dad, my brother and all the courageous
American Soldiers past and present who served and
continue to unselfishly serve the United States.
Your sacrifices are forever honored.

Contents

TURBULENT TIMES

GROWING UP

CLOSING ARGUMENT

OPENING STATEMENT

Introduction

A STORY DECADES IN THE MAKING

I am not by nature a conspiracy theorist.

I love my country. I willingly prepared to fight for the United States of America, thousands of miles away in Viet Nam.

As an attorney, I deal in facts, not supposition. Logic and reasoning are applied to guide a Trier of Fact to a just decision.

But a two-hour interview with convicted spy Joseph G. Helmich and subsequent events that I experienced had me questioning every aspect of the United States Government. It also opened old wounds.

Interview With A Spy has been an odyssey of more than 40 years, like a treasure hunt chock full of roadblocks, redactions, disinformation or flat-out denials.

Through the years, I felt like Big Brother was watching – or at least listening. Big Brother. The term became common in George Orwell's book *1984*.

The theme centered on the consequences of totalitarianism, mass surveillance and repressive regimentation of people and behaviors within society. The novel examined the role of truth and facts within societies and the ways in which they can be manipulated.

Sounds similar to what happened in the 1960s with the misinformation provided to the American public. And it sounds similar to a disturbing trend that continues to repeat itself in America.

I had unsettling vibes after traveling to a federal prison in Alabama to meet Joseph Helmich in the summer of 1982. The prison conditions, Helmich's stories and what he gave me left my shirt soaked in my own sweat. As I left the prison, I had the stunning thought of, "What the fuck did I just hear?"

During a nationally publicized Federal Court trial in Jacksonville, Florida, Joseph Helmich, a former army warrant officer, pled guilty to selling U.S. Military secrets to the Soviet Union. Helmich was given a life sentence. While in prison, he wrote his memoir. It consists of four notebooks that contain his side of the story in meticulous detail. I have safeguarded the manuscript all this time.

Through what he said and what he wrote, Helmich delivered a compelling case for how he got himself in this predicament. Not innocent but not guilty, in my view. He best described his situation as being given orders and carrying them out as any other soldier would do. He did so proudly.

Was he duped? I'll let you decide.

Supposedly groomed by his handler, an officer in the Central Intelligence Agency (CIA), Helmich played an indirect role in one of the darkest days in American history, the assassination of President John F. Kennedy.

After numerous interrogations Helmich was arrested and tried. After threats upon the lives of his wife and son, and promises of leniency if he cooperated, he pled guilty to one of the four counts of committing espionage and providing top-secret information to the Soviets. He believed that this action in pleading guilty would spare the lives of his wife and son and would lead to leniency, but instead the judge gave him a life sentence with no chance at parole.

What U.S. Government officials did to Helmich was as misleading as what it did to my generation.

In the 1960s, children of my generation were given drill instructions to "duck and cover" and to hide under our desks in the event of a nuclear attack. As if that was going to protect us.

Briefly, we felt a reprieve when President John F. Kennedy avoided a major war with the Soviet Union during the Cuban Missile Crisis and then directed the withdrawal of soldiers from Viet Nam in the process of ending the war.

After President Kennedy was assassinated in 1963, his successor, President Lyndon Johnson reversed course and ramped up the war machine in Viet Nam based upon a purported attack on a U.S. Navy vessel and on the premise of defending our national interests. It culminated in a draft – in 1969 – under new President Richard Nixon. In 1970, I was one of those in that first draft class to be drafted and inducted into the U.S. Army.

Approximately 2.7 million American service members served in Viet Nam during the war. The U.S. Military involvement began in 1961 and ended in 1975. More than 500,000 soldiers were deployed in Viet Nam during the peak years of the war. More than 58,000 died and more than 300,000 were wounded. An incalculable number of soldiers suffered from Post-Traumatic Stress Disorder while approximately 9,000 Viet Nam Veterans have sadly committed suicide.

Through a series of unexpected events, I received a deferment with conditions. Instead of shipping out to Viet Nam I found myself at Kent State. My first day of classes coincided with the return to school for a Kent State campus still feeling the effects of four university students killed and nine others injured by Ohio National Guardsmen on May 4, 1970.

The Kent State shootings played a pivotal role in triggering an end to the Viet Nam War.

It was a surreal moment in time. One minute you could be in a dorm with actress Jane Fonda, who preached her thoughts to anti-war protestors. That evening you could be in a crowd socializing outside a bar only to have a riot squad march on you and your friends to break up your gathering.

After my interview with Helmich, I left the federal prison and drove to Marietta, Georgia to visit some good friends from Kent State. On the ride to Marietta, I had flashbacks to my college days

– and the events of my youth. These memories flooded back to me during the drive and after I arrived at my friends' home. My diverse yet interconnected thoughts included:

- Kennedy speaking in my hometown
- Nuns at our school crying when hearing of Kennedy's assassination
- Lone-wolf gunman or the Deep State?
- Attending funerals of high school friends who died in Viet Nam
- The Draft Lottery
- My brave brother who fought in Viet Nam along with our neighborhood friends
- The selfless American Soldier
- My mom, bailing me out
- A college football game followed by the sight of students waving signs to end the war

We had such great hope with young President Kennedy, his beautiful wife and young children. He'd end the war in Viet Nam, bring blacks and whites closer and take us to the moon. Kennedy's reach would influence the country, the world and space.

Camelot. Our generation was ready.

Utopia lasted less than three years. Immediately after Kennedy's assassination the reality of war hit home and ramped up.

And the words of Joseph Helmich from the interview that day have continued to ring in my ears: "Coincidence is the word we use when we can't see the levers and pulleys."

I have wanted to write *Interview With A Spy* for many reasons.

Partly, I promised Joseph Helmich, and his dear wife Jean, that I would try to clear his name.

Partly, to honor the American Soldiers who fought in the Viet Nam War, especially the many who didn't return home alive.

And partly, it's provided a catharsis. I have guilt for decisions I made early in college that caused pain for my parents. I have guilt for not fighting in Viet Nam and I think about the man who replaced me. I also have guilt for not being able to help Joseph Helmich earlier. The threats made to me by the U.S. Department of Justice and the risks involved were too great to overcome at the time.

Those threats and risks no longer bind me.

Will time heal all? I'm not sure about that.

But now I can deliver on that promise made to my late client Joseph Helmich while also honoring fallen heroes.

They deserve that much.

Promises made. Promises kept.

INTERVIEW WITH A SPY

CHAPTER 1

Talladega Federal Prison

GRIM, UNSETTLING AND UNFORGETTABLE

On a beautiful, hot summer day in 1982, I pulled into the parking lot of the federal prison in Talladega, Alabama to meet and interview my prospective client, Joseph George Helmich.

I drove from Fort Myers, Florida. I couldn't afford to fly since I had just opened my own law practice earlier that year.

The Federal Correctional Institution Talladega Alabama, also known as FCI, was emblazoned on the front of the brown brick building. The building was framed with unmistakable prison security fencing.

I parked my car and turned down the radio, which blared "Eye of the Tiger." I had heard the song several times already on my way up from Fort Myers as it played on heavy rotation as a top summer hit. Not a bad song to get you pumped up for the day.

I did a final check of the background notes spread across the passenger seat that I had on Joe Helmich. I assembled that information from looking at various newspaper articles on his espionage trial.

All I knew of Joseph Helmich came from a couple of newspaper articles in *The New York Times* and *Jacksonville Times-Union*.

My knowledge was limited. The U.S. Government convicted Helmich of espionage. Helmich was Charlie Long's cellmate. I learned through my friend, Attorney Dennis Rehak, who was Charlie's criminal attorney that there were some claims that Helmich was involved with the CIA. Not much else.

So I made a call, scheduled an interview and drove to Talladega.

Like any litigator, I also looked at the questions I had compiled along with some of my random thoughts that I considered going into that interview. I then set aside those notes, looked into the rearview mirror and with my hand brushed my hair into place.

I paused and took a deep breath inside my older-model red Mercedes 450SEL that I recently bought. I couldn't afford a new Mercedes as I was only two years out of law school. I had the chance to buy this from my college roommate and brother-in-law Ron Deem, who did me a favor and sold it to me at a greatly reduced price since he already built a successful oil-and-gas business in West Virginia.

I wanted a car that made a statement and reflected my bravado as an attorney with a can't lose attitude. I was certain that this red Mercedes was it.

Before I got out, I also checked my notes to remind myself to tell Joe Helmich to say hello to his cellmate, Charlie Long.

Charlie told me about Joe through Dennis Rehak, his attorney. Dennis and I shared a small building in downtown Fort Myers at 1411 Bayview Court. Dennis had asked me to handle the real estate and business matters for the Long family, which I did well. The family approved.

Charlie was in Talladega for running a major pot smuggling operation in Southwest Florida that literally brought in a ton of marijuana through the ports and landing strips in the Everglades. Those smugglers were dubbed the 'Charlie Long Gang.'

When I got out of the car and shut the door, I caught a glimpse of myself in the tinted windows reflecting the bright Alabama sun.

With sandy, blonde hair accompanying my 6-foot, 185-pound, athletic frame, I was about 10 pounds under my playing weight when I received a full-ride, football scholarship to the University of Akron. I still felt and looked like an athlete. I always kept in shape lifting weights, running competitively in 5K races and boxing with a heavy bag hung in my garage.

I typically wear a suit and tie, but on that day, I wore a navy-blue polo shirt, tan khaki pants and boots. My mindset was that I didn't know what to expect when I went into that prison. Perhaps I would run into the 'Bad Boys of Talladega.' I was not certain.

It may sound strange if you've never been in a fight, but I knew that if I had to take care of business that day, I sure as hell wasn't going to do it wearing a lawyer's silk suit and a pair of bullshit penny loafers. That was my attitude.

I carried only a pen and a leather-bound notepad as I confidently walked toward the entrance of FCI. I ultimately would not need the pen or the paper. I did not need to take notes. The information I received would be seared into my memory forever. As I walked into FCI, I wore my confidence like an old T-shirt, well-worn and comfortable. In fact I'm known to be not just confident, but a little cocky at times.

I've always enjoyed challenges. The motto I was taught once I started organized sports in Little League baseball, CYO football and then high school and college was, "Play to Win. Never Give Up. Refuse to Lose."

I did not know it at the time but the information that I would receive that hot summer day – and after – would test that resolve. I had plenty of confidence that day, fresh off a major win against the Federal government. In one of my first cases, I represented a Florida ship captain hired to take his fishing boat to Mariel Harbor, Cuba to pick up a relative during the infamous Mariel Harbor Boatlift. The good Samaritan ship's captain I represented wound up being threatened. Facing machine gun-carrying Cuban soldiers, he had been forced to take 161 Cuban refugees back to Fort Myers Beach, Fla.

Upon my client's arrival in the United States, the government fined him $1,000 per refugee and cited him for criminal transportation of illegal aliens into this country.

Although I received a college degree in criminal justice studies, I didn't intend and never ended up practicing criminal law. However,

I was comfortable with the law and always have been one to think outside the box.

I developed a legal defense strategy against the United States Government that involved calling top government officials as key witnesses. I also would introduce the public proclamation of President Jimmy Carter to open our borders to these immigrants.

I alleged that the Carter Administration's own conduct invited and encouraged the Cuban Boat Lift. This resulted in the forced transfer of unwanted and dangerous Cubans from Castro's prisons as well as mental patients from his institutions, all mixed in with those sincere freedom-loving Cubans fleeing to America to escape the repressive Communist regime of Fidel Castro.

Does this immigration policy sound familiar?

Castro took advantage of Carter's missteps. I based my defense on an estoppel theory to show that President Carter opened the floodgates for this mass illegal immigration event by loosening immigration policies with Cuba.

President Carter did not expect that his proclamation to welcome freedom-loving Cubans to America would also open the door to some of the worst hardcore convicts in the prisons of Cuba as well as mental patients who would be released by Castro and embedded in the large group of freedom-seeking Cubans transported to the United States.

I felt strongly that Carter's missteps shouldn't be placed on the back of my client. I was willing to challenge the United States Government and do what it took to make it right for my client.

Eventually the U.S. Government recognized its failures and problematic legal position. It absolved my client of all charges with no fines imposed on him.

A big win for my client. A big win for me. As a young, fearless attorney, I demonstrated I wouldn't hesitate to challenge the actions of the President of the United States or the U.S. Government.

For that reason, I didn't think it would be a big deal to walk into FCI and interview a prospective client who I understood had his own claim of being abused by our government's intelligence agencies.

My plan? To conduct my interview, compile information and determine what I could do for him as his legal counsel. I had defeated the Department of Justice once. I prepared to do it again with this first step toward that new confrontation.

That was the plan - until it wasn't.

As I walked to the prison entrance, I realized my cockiness and confidence suddenly would be challenged. I had to suspend some of that bravado once those prison doors slammed shut behind me.

I'd never even visited a client at the county jail in Fort Myers, let alone a maximum-security section of a federal prison in Alabama. I was not used to this.

Passing through the checkpoints and security gates and hearing the noise of each door slamming shut behind me gave me a feeling of isolation from the real world. I began questioning my surroundings.

It became abundantly clear that I couldn't leave this place without permission from those running the prison. That put my ego in check.

I realized I wasn't walking with the same swagger that I entered. My pace was more measured. As a prison guest, I was led to a packed visitor room where friends and loved ones met with other prisoners. The drab institutional surroundings contrasted with the perfect Alabama summer day outside.

As I looked around, I saw a group of men who I wouldn't want to meet in a dark alley. I saw a lot of tattoos and hardcore stares in that room.

I didn't know it at the time, but FCI held more than 100 Cuban refugees/convicts who awaited deportation back to Cuba. These were some of the worst criminals Castro forced onto our shores.

The U.S. Government held them at FCI to deport them back to Cuba. The tats I saw that day on some of the prisoners in that visitors' room reflected that they were Marielitos – Cubans who emigrated during the same Mariel Harbor Boatlift incident that involved my client.

Their brands denoted criminal activity in Cuban prisons. Think of the opening scene in Scarface and the Cubans in that makeshift, fenced-in prison under the I-95 underpass in Miami. Those kinds of guys sat in that room with me.

Nine years later, in 1991, these same Cuban Marielitos led a mass riot at FCI. They took over the prison and held seven people hostage. It took 200 riot police to storm the prison to regain control and free the hostages.

This was not a place to relax or to let my guard down. That was my reality as I entered that room.

An officer directed me to move forward toward a specific table and have a seat.

For the first time I came face-to-face with my new client, inmate Joseph George Helmich – convicted Soviet spy.

CHAPTER 2

Introduction To Joseph Helmich

NINTH-GRADE DROPOUT HAD 147 IQ

Joseph Helmich stood across the table from me, a lanky red-haired guy in his mid-40s with deep-set eyes.

Helmich stared directly at me as if he could see right into my soul. He sized me up and down and waited for me to speak.

I am always observant of the other person's body language in any meeting or court proceeding. It is as important to watch their body language as it is to listen to what they say. I want to see how other people react to me, their surroundings and what is being discussed. I consider all of that in assessing a person's overall demeanor.

During that brief pause, as I looked at Helmich, I got the distinct impression that he did the same things with me.

I introduced myself as Attorney Kevin F. Jursinski.

We sat down and began the interview.

After just a few minutes, I recognized a deeply intelligent man. I later found out that he had an IQ of 147. He displayed his highly gifted intelligence during the interview. I saw a man far superior to the blue-collar convict portrayed in the press.

He was well-spoken and engaging but serious in tone. He had an agenda and attempted to convince me of his story. As my client, I had to give him the benefit of the doubt as to his claims. At the same time, I also had to maintain a lawyer's skepticism and scrutinize what he said to make sure that he was not playing me. I did not know which one was true at the time. I proceeded and kept those two parallel thoughts as I listened.

Helmich indicated that he did not want small talk. He wanted to get right down to business. It was clear that he had a story to tell, and he wanted me to be the person to help him share his story with the world.

I kept an open mind but also had to recall what I was told by my friend and criminal Attorney Dennis Rehak: "Everyone in prison believes that they are innocent."

Helmich got right to the point and stated that he worked for the U.S. Government through a Central Intelligence Agency handler that approached him in Paris while he was in the U.S. Army in his position as a crypto analyst.

That was quite a statement. He said in 1963, this CIA handler provided him with official credentials as a CIA agent. Hemich was actively recruited for his assignment by this CIA operative.

He continued and explained that he worked as an army warrant officer with the highest security clearance to receive, review and send classified military intelligence through an advanced coding system. Specifically, the army used the secret cryptograph machine identified as the KL-7.

He said the CIA knew he was stationed in a secure blockhouse just outside of Paris. He admitted that being recruited for an assignment and contributing as a CIA operative excited him. However, he didn't want to show too much eagerness in wanting the assignment.

Helmich also explained to me his backstory. He said he passed two bad checks - for $500 and $700 - to convince the Soviets that he had a motive to surrender the information.

Helmich shared the overall theme set up by his CIA handlers for this mission: The Soviets would never believe the information if

Helmich handed it to them. They needed to be convinced Helmich had a motive for surrendering the secrets. The Soviets would believe it if they paid for it and felt they stole it.

The cover story that he had bad debts was a contrived and well-thought-out backstory based upon the spycraft training the CIA handler provided him. This was not an act of desperation over a few bad checks. Helmich was smart, analytical and had a grasp of world events.

The CIA didn't come to Helmich's defense during his trial and conviction of working for the Soviets. He explained that he had a hard time accepting that he might have been used by the Soviets, the CIA (or both) and had actually been their patsy. However, his current reality was a conviction and life sentence.

I don't think his ego or pride would allow him to accept this as true, although he did admit that after his trial started, he began to question what was real and what wasn't.

Helmich also did not want to accept that he might have been a pawn in a larger and more sinister political chess match. He then questioned whether his recruitment was by:

A) The Soviets with a false CIA front?

B) Soviet moles in the CIA?

C) The CIA as he originally thought.

Helmich spent the last six months contemplating these thoughts as to the possible disinformation these entities gave him. Those thoughts had begun to haunt him especially when he realized that he was part of a major world event.

Even with all these doubts rolling around in his head, Helmich remained confident as he continued explaining the intricate plan that he was taught to carry out.

As I listened to his description of the events, one thing became abundantly clear: He showed no remorse. He did not apologize. Methodical and descriptive, he displayed no sorrow for what he did, but in fact, emphatically asserted that he took on an assignment to transfer top-secret coding information to the Soviets and executed exactly what his CIA handler taught him to do.

The lack of remorse resembled the description I would read later in the trial transcripts about him. The U.S. Attorney railed on Helmich about this in the sentencing hearing. He also annoyed the trial judge because he said he planned to write a book about his experience in the U.S. Army.

During our interview, Helmich's calm demeanor and matter of fact speaking appeared as if he wanted to give me a lecture on how to be a master spy and how he infiltrated the Soviets by convincing them that he was helping them instead of manipulating them.

Helmich had a mission and fulfilled it. Simple as that. He did not express regret. He did what he was ordered to do. He would now serve the rest of his life in prison for these actions. He could not reconcile that in his mind. He uttered the word "patsy" more than once as he described how he may have been set up and played in this entire scenario.

Nonetheless, Helmich presented himself as one cool, confident spy. This description contradicted what I read in the newspaper articles in preparation for the interview. I didn't expect or prepare for this at all. As this interview unfolded, I recognized my reality and adapted accordingly.

Helmich boastfully explained that the main reason the CIA chose him to do the covert operations came about because of his high intelligence and top-secret clearance in the United States Army as a warrant officer. Working in a blockhouse outside of Paris gave him access to the Soviet Embassy and the Soviet Trade Mission in Paris. Helmich transmitted top-level security messages through the KL-7, which had the nickname "Adonis."

The National Security Agency (NSA) developed it. The U.S. Military used the then state-of-the-art decoding machine to protect our top-secret communications. Helmich claimed that due to his IQ, acumen at his job and security position, the CIA identified him as a perfect person to use in their espionage efforts against the Soviets. The agency selected and groomed him for this mission, he said. The best of the best.

As he spoke, Helmich kept his hands on four notebooks in front of him. He didn't open them but kept them guarded and close. He explained that he wrote his memoir about his time in the military as a spy. He emphasized that he was not a lone-wolf spy. He refuted what I related in the newspaper stories that his desperation to obtain payments for secrets became the motive for his actions. Helmich had another reason for telling his story. It was buried when he confessed and never took the stand in his own defense. He related to me that he was coerced into accepting the plea bargain based upon threats he received that his family would be murdered if he took the stand in his own defense.

At Helmich's sentencing hearing, not only was the U.S. Attorney who was prosecuting the case clearly upset with Helmich planning to give an interview and write a book, but so was Federal Judge Susan Black.

Judge Black listened to Helmich's position when he confessed and reminded him of the seriousness of his offense. She then did just the opposite of what Helmich thought would happen based upon his anticipated plea bargain. Rather than show some leniency, she came down as hard as she possibly could against Helmich and stated on the record:

"Congress has expressed its view of the seriousness of the offense, and the Court can only speak through its sentence as to the seriousness of the offense and that sentence will be for the maximum penalty provided by law.

"It is adjudged that the defendant is hereby committed to the custody of the Attorney General or his authorized representative for imprisonment for the remainder of his natural life." [2-1]

Judge Black further went on to express her outrage that Helmich would consider publishing his memoir and possibly disclosed this entire plot in an interview with NBC after the trial. She was one displeased Federal Court Judge.

However, it also raised the question: Why plead to a maximum life sentence rather than take a chance on presenting your defense? The loss at a full-blown trial actually could be no worse than the plea deal Helmich accepted. Helmich would never see the outside world again, one life sentence, three life sentences or 30. It made no sense other than Helmich's explanation of the threats to the lives of his wife and son.

Sitting there, I had the feeling he always thought he was the smartest guy in the room. In fact, in most rooms he may have been just that. That intelligence, along with the necessary training provided to pull off the treasonous act, resulted in one of the most significant transfers of military coding secrets in U.S. history.

Presidential Bombshell

Now behind bars, Helmich's motivation to share his story grew.

By delivering to the Soviets a cryptograph machine and supplying them with the constantly changing codes, he provided them with top-secret information at one of the most critical times in United States history - the assassination of President John F. Kennedy.

Once these codes were deciphered, the Soviets would know the when, where, why and how regarding all the United States top-secret military plans during the limited time period that the codes would be in effect.

Helmich explained that this was especially important when it came to having knowledge of the plan of action (or lack thereof) by the United States toward the Soviets immediately after the Kennedy Assassination. If the United States blamed the Soviets for the assassination and retaliated, perhaps that would have started World War III.

I found Helmich's story riveting. The information and the timing of these events seemed dramatic and for me filled in a missing part of the facts around the Kennedy assassination. I noticed my elevating pulse and I felt myself taking a deep breath as I absorbed all this information.

At one point, I looked around the room to see if anyone else was listening since what I heard sounded significant and damning. Helmich unloaded quite the information dump.

This background supported the conspiracy theories that have

swirled around the Kennedy Assassination. It came directly from a source, the spy convicted of this very act, which was the delivery of the top-secret coding information to the Soviets on the day after the assassination. Helmich's assignment to transfer the top-secret codes was planned months in advance. I leaned in and asked more questions.

As he responded Helmich stopped and asked, "Are you all right?"

He must have sensed some uneasiness although I acted as calm as one could under these circumstances.

He asked me why I was sweating. I never even noticed. I looked down and I pitted out as though I had just finished a workout. The adrenalin rush, the information dropped on me in that interview as well as that prison environment caused me to sweat even though I outwardly acted calm.

My response to Helmich: "I'm fine - it's just a little hot in here."

He looked at me and knew I hadn't told him the truth, but he continued. The Alabama heat and humidity in that room did not cause me to react. The penetrating information he provided me in that environment brought up my heartbeat and tension level.

Helmich just told me that the people and organization that he worked for knew well in advance of what was to take place on November 22, 1963. Helmich played an integral part in the plan.

The U.S. Government had this front and center in its indictment of Helmich, charging him with transferring military secrets to the Soviets in the "Fall of 1963." It convicted Helmich of this very act based upon a surprising confession and plea deal that occurred after presenting its case but before Helmich could present his defense.

That confession made no logical sense at that point in his trial. But the confession to what the U.S. Government alleged does not diminish the espionage act he was charged with at the time of the Kennedy Assassination.

Helmich again confirmed to me the CIA order: To provide the Soviets immediate access to U.S. Military codes for the days following Nov. 22, 1963. As I sat there and he revealed this information to me, I realized, if true, that Helmich's transfer of

U.S. Military codes played a small role in the international conspiracy to assassinate President John F. Kennedy. By the Soviets being able to read our codes the days following the Kennedy assassination they would absolutely be able to verify that there would be no U.S. reprisals against the Soviets. That closed the circle on the issue.

If true, the U.S. Government - through its intelligence agencies, the Soviets or both - clearly knew about the event well before it happened.

Knowledge before the act makes it a conspiracy to murder the then President of the United States.

I was absolutely stunned as to what I just heard.

2-1: Page 45 lines 14-18 Transcript of Sentencing before the Honorable Judge Black October 16, 1981

CHAPTER 3

Major Piece Of Assassination Puzzle

HELMICH'S ACTIONS A BIG REVELATION TO A TRAGIC DAY IN AMERICAN HISTORY

I just couldn't believe what Joseph Helmich told me.

But he kept coming with more information.

When I found my voice, I asked Helmich if he realized what he was alleging.

He said that he absolutely knew what he was alleging because he knew it to be true. He also said that he voluntarily provided the Federal Bureau of Investigation (FBI) with the same information, which included the sell-off of military codes and equipment to the Soviets. That transfer of top-secret codes began before the Kennedy Assassination and culminated on Nov. 23, 1963, the day after he was killed.

Helmich said he provided this information to the FBI when it interrogated him before his arrest, certain that his CIA handlers would come to the rescue.

That never happened.

The U.S. Government indicted and convicted him in a high-profile federal trial for acts of espionage. These same acts were the reason he sat across from me that day at FCI Talladega.

As I listened to the impactful information that I received in that drab environment, I began to understand the significance of what I heard. This was definitely the high-level intelligence information turnover as the U.S. Government charged in its indictment of Helmich.

But the U.S. Government buried the headline as its language stated the espionage acts occurred in the "Fall of 1963." As Helmich related, the government didn't ask the specific date when he turned over key codes to the Soviets. Why did the prosecution not advance the date that it actually occurred? Were they warned not to?

Looking back, the sell-off of military secrets to the Soviets in the days following Kennedy's assassination seemed relevant and a pivotal date to broaden the net of others involved.

The FBI apparently did not think the specific date was relevant or that it could help it convict Helmich. Significant evidence. Hidden in plain sight.

I asked Helmich to explain in more detail how he knew a conspiracy had taken place to assassinate Kennedy.

Helmich leaned back in his chair, crossed his arms, and with a smug look on his face told me, "I knew. Because of the role I had played in it."

He began telling me what he had experienced and what he was directed to do by his CIA handler in the days and months before Nov. 22. Helmich explained that he was stationed in the U.S. - Fort Bragg, N.C. - in early November 1963 when his CIA handler directed him to prepare to fly to Paris later that month. His handler would let him know the exact date but certainly toward the end of November. As it turns out the 'go date' was Nov. 22, 1963, the day of the assassination.

I pressed Helmich on the timing of his assignments and asked him whether the date of his assignment could have been a coincidence with the Kennedy assassination?

Helmich responded to me with a quote his CIA contacts gave him: "Coincidence is the word we use when we can't see the levers and pulleys."

When I pressed him on the events he was involved in and the possible coincidental timing of his actions and the Kennedy Assassination, he smirked at the suggestion. He made me feel like my question was naïve.

"Read your history," he told me. "Great world events just don't occur by happenstance."

Then he described his assignment: CIA officials ordered Helmich to deliver to the Soviet GRU a briefcase containing the current top-secret codes to go along with the KL-7 equipment that Helmich had already sold them.

Why? Helmich advised me that the Soviet GRU was that country's military intelligence agency, the counterpart to our military intelligence. It was a much larger organization than the KGB. He told me that everyone automatically thinks KGB but GRU was more powerful.

As expected, Helmich received the phone call that confirmed he was to board a flight to Paris on Nov. 22 to complete his mission. His handler insisted that Helmich be on an early flight on his way to Orly Airport in Paris.

To further camouflage his trip, Helmich invited his wife, Jean, to go with him. He said she had been looking forward to returning to Paris and spending some quality time together with him. Helmich recalled sitting on the plane en route to Paris via New York City and her telling him about how happy she was because her life now seemed perfect.

They were flying over rural Virginia when the pilot came over the intercom and made a shocking announcement. The pilot announced that President John F. Kennedy had been assassinated in Dallas.

Helmich said both he and Jean were devastated. Many of the passengers sobbed and were visibly upset. No one wanted to believe it. Upon landing in New York, Helmich promptly called his handler and asked if he should return home.

The handler said, "Absolutely not."

In fact, the handler sternly ordered Helmich to proceed to Paris.

His handler insisted that Helmich complete his mission and deliver the current secret codes to the Soviets.

Helmich did not know the full significance of transferring the codes that morning but after the pilot's announcement of Kennedy's death, he began to realize he was a part of a much larger plan.

The immediate delivery of our top-secret military codes directly to the GRU after the assassination would let the Soviets know that the United States, the superpower and direct enemy of the Soviets, was not going to react or retaliate against them in any way after Kennedy's death.

The transfer of the then-current crypto codes enabled the Soviets to view top-secret U.S. Military communications at the time and determine that the United States would not launch an attack that could start World War III.

There would be no retaliation - and no WWIII - if the CIA convinced the Soviets that the plot was orchestrated by members of the United States own intelligence agencies. If this is true, then there were forces at play who knew that the assassination would take place well before it happened.

Helmich's delivery of the top-secret information became an important piece of a much larger puzzle surrounding these well-planned events in a coup d'etat of the President of the United States.

Helmich performed his part.

He delivered the top-secret documents and current coding information to the Soviets in Paris just after the assassination. The Soviets awarded Helmich the Medal of Lenin for his great service to the communist state, praised him and gave him the rank of colonel in the Soviet Army. They told Helmich he would be recognized by the Soviets as a true hero.

The honors clearly reflected the importance the Soviets felt for Helmich surrendering secure information that enabled them to monitor U.S. Military communications during that critical time after the assassination.

The Soviets paid him $131,000 for his services. This payment in 1963 is equivalent to $1.3 million in 2025 and also reinforced the significance to the Soviets of what Helmich delivered them.

Helmich acted out his role well in this tragic play on one of the worst days in American history.

CHAPTER 4

Disinformation

THE NEWS AND NARRATIVE LABELS
HELMICH AS A LONE-WOLF TRAITOR

As I interviewed Joseph Helmich, I reflected on the research that I obtained before I arrived. Clearly what I heard that day wasn't what I read.

Back in the day, doing research on people and events differed a lot. We did not have Google at our fingertips.

While law firms had computers, they were not tied into internet search engines.

There was access to rudimentary research but nothing like what we now have.

One way we researched national or international events was to go to the public library and pull up microfilm copies of newspaper articles. I read *The New York Times* on the start of the Helmich prosecution and trial as well as the *Jacksonville Times-Union.*

The Times article on the Helmich trial published on September 22, 1981 coincided with my 31st birthday. It referenced that Helmich quit school in the ninth grade, joined the army in 1954 and ultimately became a top crypto custodian with the highest military clearance. It seemed odd the paper inferred that was the natural progression of a soldier with only a middle school education.

The focus of *The Times* article on the ninth-grade dropout angle made Helmich out as a misfit. Conveniently, the article glossed over the fact that Helmich had a superior intelligence since that did not fit the story it sold as a lone-wolf traitor. First point I learned: the article portrayed Helmich inaccurately.

What I quickly learned in my discussion - and as I later discovered with more research - was that over a 10-year period, Helmich rapidly advanced through the military ranks to his position of a warrant officer and a crypto custodian with top-secret clearance. I learned his meteoric rise put Helmich personally in charge of the, "...custody, handling, safeguarding and destruction of military code-making materials," as alleged by the U.S. Government in its indictment. Considered the top cryptographer in his unit, he was well-regarded by his commanding officer.

Amazing resume and position achieved by someone with only a middle school education. This significant information was never mentioned in *The Times* article. I've always had a healthy distrust for what the news media portrays as accurate. Perhaps this information was leaked to the press to spin a narrative to discredit Helmich.

The Times article went on to indicate that the indictment of Helmich charged him with selling and providing the Soviets the entire KL-7 crypto system as part of a significant espionage event. The article stated that he did so in a secret meeting at the Soviet Embassy and the Soviet Trade Mission in Paris in the Fall of 1963, the same phrase used in the trial proceeding. Why not state that it was done on Nov. 22, 1963? The Soviets paid Helmich $131,000, per the allegations made in the Court filings and the information advanced by the FBI.

What *The Times* article did not elaborate on was the alleged payment, which was a phenomenal amount of money for the transfer of these secrets. The initial reports on the famous Rosenberg trial was that they received $1 million from their sale of atomic secrets to the Soviets. However, later reports indicated the Rosenbergs were paid significantly less. The payment to Helmich was a historic payment for top-secret information reflecting the importance of what the Soviets received. A major fact glossed over.

The Times article went on to indicate that Helmich was oddly, "under suspicion for 17 years," but the FBI would not reveal why he was not charged until 1981. In fact, the trial transcript that I read years later showed the FBI never had any information to charge Helmich, other than the information Helmich had voluntarily provided to them. In almost 17 years, they could not assemble enough of a case file to charge Helmich?

The FBI, like the U.S. Army, identified in the trial court documents, only knew that Helmich had one of the highest security clearances for his position and it was reported he spent quite a bit of money. Neither the U.S. Army at the time, nor the FBI over nearly a two-decade investigation period, could turn up any evidence to charge Helmich on anything, let alone a complicated espionage plot of this magnitude.

The Times article pointed out that Helmich voluntarily met with the FBI an amazing nine times before they charged him. The article also stated that Helmich, who debriefed the bureau on all of his activities, was afraid he would go to jail if he did not cooperate.

Being afraid he would go to jail apparently meant that Helmich was not smart enough to get legal advice or consider the implications of his debriefing the FBI over the course of a year.

Helmich was one of the brightest people I have ever interviewed. With an IQ of 147, access to substantial amounts of tax-free cash, logically Helmich could have easily retained legal counsel to advise him on how he should conduct himself. Helmich admitted to me in our interview that he did voluntarily cooperate with the FBI.

Helmich still tightly clutched the four bound notebooks.

It appeared the story he wanted me to know would not end after our conversation.

CHAPTER 5

The Manuscript

HELMICH REVEALS ALL IN METICULOUS DETAIL

Joseph Helmich suggested that before I left, I should browse through the four bound notebooks he presented to me.

The notepads all had brown covers enclosing white-lined writing paper. They were something you'd see in an office supply store in the 1980s.

Written in ink with large, stenciled-style letters across each of the booklets was the title *KAK* with the names of the cities where Helmich carried on his espionage activities.

The first notebook had a white mailing label at the bottom of the cover noting Joseph G. Helmich, CIA as the author with a copyright symbol before the year 1982. The second through fourth of the notebooks also had typewritten labels that listed the following:

KAK/KAK
COPYWRITE APPLIED FOR 1982
KEVIN JURINSKI, ESQUIRE FOR
JOSEPH G. HELMICH, AUTHOR
Copywrite applied for on affidavit

When I saw the labels, it struck me that before our interview, he had already determined he would entrust me with his story since the front stickers had my name on them (even though my last name and copyright were misspelled).

As we talked, I opened the first notebook for a cursory leaf through of what was before me, as Helmich suggested. These booklets were not typed but handwritten. In pencil and ink. With no strikethroughs.

Who can write hundreds of pages in long hand with no strikethroughs? My first reaction was that only someone of extreme intelligence could organize all these thoughts in his mind and then hand write out hundreds of pages of details with minimal edits. That writing proficiency reflected someone with extreme analytical skills and detailed expression. This was a ninth-grade dropout?

The first few paragraphs of the first chapter caught my eye. It started with Helmich's recollection of the tense and voluminous military-code traffic occurring during the Cuban Missile Crisis.

I mentioned this to Helmich. He indicated information he received and transmitted during the crisis in 1962 was clearly more ominous than what President Kennedy told the public. Helmich expressed how close we came to World War III. This information, had it been released, could have set off a worldwide panic.

Those opening paragraphs revealed his insider knowledge. Helmich described his position to observe all these activities and communications. A peak behind the curtain, if you will.

Privy to military intelligence traffic, Helmich had the distinct impression that our military leaders questioned the leadership and goals of President Kennedy before and during the Bay of Pigs Invasion and the Cuban Missile Crisis.

Pretty powerful insight. I looked forward to reading the manuscript in detail after I left FCI Talladega.

New Legislation

Helmich paused and told me something I did not know.

He said new federal legislation passed after his trial. He indicated that such legislation was in place to protect disclosure of CIA operatives' names and practices. The legislation intended to block any information that could result in these operatives' identities being disclosed.

After the interview, I learned that Congress passed an amendment to the National Security Act of 1947. This occurred within six months of Helmich's conviction.

The new legislation was titled the *Intelligence Identities Protection Act of 1982*. This established criminal penalties for any person who knowingly disclosed information, which identified a U.S. covert intelligence agent.

Had Helmich put on his defense rather than accepting a plea, he would have been able to get his story out without restriction. Now, this new legislation would prevent him from releasing the names of the actual CIA agents he claimed he worked with and forever sealed any effort on his part to clear his name.

As mentioned at the sentencing hearing, Judge Susan Black herself warned Helmich about writing a book about his espionage activities. She also indicated that if Helmich wrote a book, all profits would go to the U.S. Government.

Helmich assured me that his manuscript identified the exact name and rank of every Soviet military officer or agent with whom he came in contact as well as the precise date, time and location of all meetings, secret drop locations and other spycraft he was taught.

However, Helmich indicated he changed the names of CIA operatives that he dealt with, although the dates, times and locations of all those contacts were specific. He emphasized the names of the Soviets were accurate as to their military rank and reflected the trust the Soviets had in him over the numerous meetings that took place.

Helmich took risks and put himself out there by taking all of these chances. I never once got the impression that the money he made was a major factor or any factor at all in why he accepted this assignment. Helmich was motivated by the chance, as he related, to participate in a role with the CIA and serve his country as he had been doing for the past 10 years.

Helmich warned me in advance that he took precautions to avoid releasing the names of the CIA operatives who he claimed to be working for. Helmich explained he wanted the facts to come out without revealing the CIA operatives' names. He realized that still might create an issue with the manuscript release.

However, if the FBI and the U.S. Government were correct that he was a lone-wolf actor that only handed over documents to the Soviets, how could Helmich have the names, identities and operational information of specific CIA officers or operatives? Why would the Soviets give him that information? And if the Soviets did not, how was Helmich supposed to have knowledge of specific CIA agents in the field unless he was working with those CIA agents?

KAK Meaning

Helmich told me why he titled the manuscript *KAK*. In Russian, *KAK* (pronounced "kahk") means "how." It is a common Russian word used to ask about the manner or method of doing something. This was Helmich's method or the "how." Helmich filled in blanks on the Kennedy Assassination and gave a behind-the-scenes look at the "how" and opened the door to the questions of "who" was behind this and "why?"

We already knew the "what, where and when" answers of the Kennedy Assassination in Dallas on Nov. 22, 1963. The "how" of the plan demonstrated that this was well orchestrated in advance and involved numerous players on various levels.

We discussed that Helmich wanted his manuscript published to explain to the public what role he played in these events. It's a story the FBI prevented him from giving at his trial because of threats to his family.

As we were concluding the interview, Helmich told me that he felt betrayed by the CIA. Helmich expressed his feelings that the CIA either duped, betrayed or made him a scapegoat for his spy mission. Or that he really was unwittingly recruited to be a Soviet spy, perhaps by a Soviet mole in the CIA and that he was manipulated by the Soviets in a plot to deliver them top-secret information.

Why didn't the FBI explore all those issues? As he sat there for the first time in the interview Helmich seemed vulnerable – and uncertain of who had shaped his fate.

That thought haunted him, which he lamented in his *KAK: Manuscript* that I would read and re-read to fully digest all the information Helmich provided in great detail.

Helmich seemed conflicted as to whether he was recruited by the CIA as he believed or he was played like a pawn in a larger chess match, then removed from the board when he was no longer useful, or his information could prove problematic for someone. What he wrote in his notebooks summarized his internal conflict. Helmich also wrote that when he was arrested, he felt "completely deserted and betrayed."

"What I fear most is that "XXXX," "XXXX" and even "XXXX" were the moles themselves," he wrote. "It would answer all my questions. That is except for one. If they were Soviet agents, then why in hell did they want me to go into Russia?

"And if they were or anyone of them was, then it means the Russians did assassinate Kennedy - that would make me feel a lot better than the fear I've lived with all these years, that the CIA killed him as the facts point to."

His manuscript reinforced the uncertainties he expressed to me.

Yet, sitting across from him in that prison, I tried to process the impactful information I was hearing at that moment. It was a mountain of information to take in.

Helmich made me promise that I would help him get his story out with the idea that the proceeds from his *KAK: Manuscript* would go to assist his family and that if I was successful to accept a percentage of those proceeds.

He apparently had second thoughts about his strategy to remain silent. He told me he anticipated a reduced sentence, not what he received. His wife was promised financial support as part of the bargain for him to plead out. That also didn't happen.

I sat across from Helmich that hot summer day in Alabama as we talked through these events in FCI Talladega. Toward the end of the meeting, Helmich looked me in the eye and asked me to assist him.

I agreed that I would help him and accepted Joseph G. Helmich as a client.

This was one impactful interview.

Helmich also warned me to protect myself and indicated that there were forces that would block my efforts. I did not grasp the full extent of his warning. I did realize that I was in possession of an important written work that revealed information that could prove to be insightful to the Kennedy Assassination and perhaps damaging to our intelligence agencies. I felt the weight of that responsibility. I understood what I had to do and also recognized Helmich's warning. I would soon find out what that meant in the coming month.

Parting Looks

We shook hands and I said goodbye.

As I left, I turned around to see Helmich heading back toward the door to his cell block. He also turned, looked back at me and nodded.

The interview moved me.

As I finally made my way out of the doors of FCI Talladega carrying those notebooks, I took a deep breath of the clean Alabama air and felt the summer sun on my face. Most of all I felt – freedom!

As I got to my car, I paused, took another deep breath. I took off my sweaty polo shirt and stuck it in the back window. I hoped it would dry on my way to Marietta, Georgia where I went to see two of my best friends from Kent State.

I would need a drink when I arrived.

I did not have a briefcase with me to store the notebooks – only the pad and pen I brought in, neither of which I used.

I did not need to take notes. What I heard that day has been seared into my memory.

I opened the car door and reached into the glove compartment. I took out the Mercedes car service manual, which was in a black leather case and tossed the service manual back into the glove compartment. I replaced the car service manual with the four notebooks.

Amazingly, they fit precisely into the black leather case as if the case was designed to hold them. I still have the manuscript in that black Mercedes case, stored securely. Copies are also stored in other discreet locations for additional protection.

I jumped into the Mercedes and started the car. I took another deep breath and looked out into the blue Alabama afternoon sky.

CHAPTER 6

The Drive To Marietta

PROCESSING THE INTERVIEW AND REMEMBERING PRESIDENT KENNEDY

As I pulled out of the parking lot that afternoon at FCI with my sweaty Polo shirt hanging out the back window to dry, I drew the attention of departing prison visitors. That did not phase me. My thoughts focused on my interview with Joseph Helmich:

What the fuck did I just hear? And what the hell am I going to read in those four handwritten notebooks that make up the manuscript?

Did I just hear information that could be relevant to answering some of the conspiracy questions on the assassination of President Kennedy?

Who else knows what I just heard?

How the hell do I explain this?

What do I do with this information and the manuscript?

This was a major goddamn thing. A warrant officer with top-secret clearance. CIA allegations. Convicted Soviet spy. The espionage mission as part of the design for the event of the century planned well in advance.

The Kennedy Assassination. A lot of thoughts swirled in my head on that drive to Marietta, Georgia.

As I drove, I kept having flashbacks to President John F. Kennedy, going back to my Catholic elementary school days in the 1960s. That wonderful and idyllic time in America. A new, young and vibrant President with an equally young and beautiful wife now at the head of the U.S. Government.

Jack and Jackie. The new Camelot. The age of the Innocence. Or so it seemed.

I just turned 10 years old in late September 1960 when John F. Kennedy visited my hometown of Lorain, Ohio. He gave a campaign speech at George Daniel Field, a stadium in our city where I would eventually play my high school football games.

It was at George Daniel Field in front of a standing room only crowd in 1967 when my team, the undefeated Lorain St. Mary Fighting Irish, beat the previously undefeated and rival Elyria Catholic Panthers for the conference championship for the second year in a row.

For Kennedy's campaign speech that day, George Daniel Stadium was far more crowded than our standing room only championship game. My parents took me to the event but it was so crowded we could not get into the stadium. Spectators jammed the entrances.

Lorain is a blue-collar steel town on the shores of Lake Erie. In the 1960s, it was heavily Democratic with a high percentage of Catholics, like my parents and their friends. Everyone was excited that the possible future President was visiting our city. This is similar to what we have seen with Donald Trump's campaign rallies and the massive attendance records for those events in both 2016 and 2020.

That day outside the stadium, all I could do was stand on the street with Mom and Dad in that overflow crowd outside of the stadium and try to catch a few words from Kennedy's speech. We heard the loud cheers as he concluded. I looked up to see the look on my parents' faces and they seemed so happy and proud. Everything seemed so perfect. Standing there on the street outside the stadium, we were hoping to get a glimpse of this man who would be king.

As we stood there, we did get to see the Kennedy motorcade as it left George Daniel Field, passing us by on Oberlin Avenue as they headed west to Elyria, Ohio.

On my drive to Marietta after meeting Helmich, I reflected on the Kennedy motorcade as it passed us by that day in Lorain outside the stadium. I wondered what those spectators felt standing on the street surrounding Dealey Plaza as the motorcade passed them by that fateful day in Dallas.

Did they have the same joy and hope on their faces that I saw on the face of my parents? And the same anticipation of having the privilege to get a glimpse of the President?

What did they feel as they watched Kennedy's head get blown off in that violent act? How do you ever erase that from your memory? What do you do years later in the middle of the night when those demons invade your dreams?

I continued driving and thought about what Helmich told me. In my mind's eye I was seeing the Zapruder film all over again. As I drove down the highway, I became emotional thinking about what I heard in my interview with Helmich and how it related to the planning of the Kennedy Assassination. Tears came to my eyes as I remembered that tragic day. How could that have happened? Who were these men that planned and carried out this assassination?

I tried to unravel what Helmich just told me. Knowing that Kennedy's brutal murder was known and planned in advance, perhaps by our own CIA or our intelligence community, got me very angry. At the same time tears streamed down my cheeks as I recalled Kennedy's head exploding as he sat next to his wife.

I gripped the steering wheel as I drove. I don't recall ever crying while at the same time being so very angry.

Heading toward Marietta on Interstate 20, I continued having flashbacks to the Kennedy years, going back to my Catholic school days. The nuns in my Catholic grade school were oh so proud. The first Catholic President. As a Catholic, he was one of us! After he was elected, some of the nuns kidded me about my initials being just like JFK's. Of course, my initials KFJ (Kevin Francis Jursinski) are the reverse of JFK's.

As I continued my drive through a slow turn to get off I-20, I just could not get Helmich's thoughts out of my head. I flashed back again to the haunting Zapruder film showing the Kennedy motorcade and their own slow turn through Dealey Plaza that fateful sunny Friday afternoon in Dallas to set up the kill shot on Kennedy. Man, that ride to Marietta was intense with all of those thoughts of the Kennedy Assassination.

My head was pounding.

I then had a feeling that I never had before — being utterly alone and helpless in a violent world now realizing there were powerful forces within America that actually controlled major national events.

I realized that we as citizens don't have the control we grew up believing we had. And this influential group, called the Deep State in today's parlance, is powerful enough to direct or influence our national policies, to the extent of orchestrating the assassination of our then-sitting U.S. President to effect regime change to enable them to ramp up and prosecute the Viet Nam War?

I reflected on my interview as I drove. It confirmed in my mind what was just previously whispered for fear of being labeled a conspiracy advocate — John F. Kennedy was assassinated in a planned and staged coup d'etat by a group of unknown individuals in our intelligence services and perhaps supported by the Deep State.

The assassination was planned and for a designated purpose. Kennedy's assassination was not simply some random act by a purported lone-wolf gunman. My interview with Helmich, my review of his manuscript and the entire trial file solidified my belief in the conspiracy to assassinate the then-sitting President of the United States.

It was early evening when I finally arrived at my long-time friend's home in Marietta. I pulled into the driveway. What a long and emotional ride. I noted that I had not even played the radio during my drive since I was caught up in my own thoughts.

I realized I had to pull myself together from an emotional day. I needed to calm down and try and enjoy what was left of the evening with my friends.

So caught up in my thoughts, I realized I still had no shirt on. I pulled out a clean shirt since my polo shirt in the back window was still not wearable. I took the carrying case containing the notebooks and stuck it into my overnight bag.

My friends' welcoming porch light was on. I got out of the car and headed to their front door hoping for some friendship and a strong drink after a long day.

CHAPTER 7

Glory Days

GOOD FRIENDS, GOOD DRINKS
AND UNFORGETTABLE MEMORIES

It was one long day followed by a long drive with a lot of emotions. I was looking forward to seeing my old friends from Kent State, George and Gloria Cappellini. George opened the front door to greet me. I walked up to them and gave them both a big hug and headed inside. I needed those hugs.

I looked forward to unwinding, but the first thing I did was to take a minute and call my wife Darlene to tell her that I arrived safely at George and Gloria's house. I told her that I had a lot to share with her when I got back home, too much to discuss in a phone call and told her I loved her as I ended the call.

I then had a few drinks with George and Gloria and talked about the current success they were both having in their careers. I shared with them the first year of my solo law practice. They asked about my Darlene, who was also a good friend to George and Gloria. Darlene and I met George and Gloria when we were at Kent State and have been good friends since then.

I looked forward to unwinding. We had a few drinks and talked about the current success they were both having in their careers. I shared with them the first year of my solo law practice. They asked about my wife Darlene, who was also a good friend to George and Gloria having met them when we were all at Kent.

We also talked about our old friends from Kent State and the good times we had there. We did not want to slide into a conversation about our glory days, but as we talked and drank, we agreed that no one could match what we did at Kent State in the turbulent times we experienced. Given what I heard today, I thought the look back on our college years was poignant, especially since a great deal of the time we spent at Kent was affected by the loom of the Viet Nam War and the anti-war protests on the Kent State campus and nationally. Kent was the epicenter of the anti-war movement against the Viet Nam War, a war that might have never been had Kennedy not been assassinated.

What an interesting time to be in college and at Kent State in particular during a major shift in American society, in part fueled by the war protests and specifically the on-campus killings at Kent State of student protestors. In the Spring of 1970 the world saw the Ohio National Guard march onto the Kent State campus during a beautiful sunny day, Monday, May 4, 1970, only to shoot and kill four students and bystanders during a peaceful campus protest. My brother-in-law Ron Deem was on the Kent Commons heading to a final exam. He witnessed the murder of four students that day by our own soldiers. He can never erase that memory and can only be thankful that he was not a casualty.

The next fall, the beautiful campus in Kent, Ohio, generally regarded previously as a Mid-American conference party school, erupted into ground zero for the anti-Viet Nam War protest movement. We attracted every far-left organization in America. We became the Berkeley of the Midwest.

There was always an underlying tone at Kent with the clash of law and order opposing the freedom of being at a university and growing up in America. It was hard to reconcile the horrific shootings.

The Kennedy Assassination was a major turning point in America as were the anti-war protests against the Viet Nam War. That ended the innocence in America and created the reason why most Americans do not trust our government.

Such an emotionally odd time: Some of our brothers and friends were sacrificing their lives fighting the Viet Nam War half a world away, while some of our other friends were protesting that same war Kennedy wanted to avoid. Looking back, had Kennedy lived he may have been the only person in America powerful enough to be the champion to both of those disparate groups.

There were amazing nightly activities both on and off campus. There were war protests followed by police riot teams marching down the main streets of Kent to break up any assembly of people. Downtown Kent is where all the bars were located. Exiting a Water Street bar after catching a set from Joe Walsh and the James Gang, you'd have an equal chance of scoring a Quaalude or a joint as you would have a chance of being swept up in a forced police march.

Police, dressed in full riot gear, spanned the full width of the street from store front to store front. They would sweep the streets breaking up any small group of students, regardless of their intentions. Generally on Water Street it was to get high and have some fun, but the riot squad did not stop to inquire. This went on for two years at the campus.

While the protests and demonstrations occurred, our Kent State football team was enjoying its best years ever with the ushering in of the Coach Don James era in 1971. The legendary coach guided the Kent State team from 1971 to 1974. Kent State enjoyed the best teams it ever had, winning the Mid America Conference while being led by future NFL Hall of Fame linebacker Jack Lambert and an Olympic sprinter at wide receiver in Gerald Tinker. Both became second-round NFL draft picks.

Don James went on to great success at the University of Washington with his team sharing the title of National Champion in 1991. One of Coach James' graduate assistants, Nick Saban, became a legendary college coach. Nick was a recent Kent State graduate who started his coaching career at Kent. I never met Coach Saban while at Kent. Years later while I was an NFL agent I had the opportunity to have an insightful phone call with Coach

Saban about one of his players that I represented who went on to become a first round draft pick of the Minnesota Vikings. Coach Saban was also a star on the Kent teams along with Gary Pinkel, who went on to a successful coaching career at Missouri before he retired in Southwest Florida.

So, picture yourself as a Kent State student going to a football game at the stadium on the Kent campus on a sunny Saturday afternoon. Then leaving the game and perhaps participating in an anti-war protest late that evening after speakers such as Jane Fonda, Dick Gregory and Jerry Rubin, the leader of the Students for a Democratic Society (SDS) visited our Kent campus. Kent State was then identified as the hot bed for the Viet Nam protests with these speakers' appearances designed to spike protests on the Viet Nam War and other social issues.

In the midst of these events, George and I became entrepreneurs at Kent State. We were involved in a number of money-making projects at Kent. Among those ventures, we started a concert promotion company and had some modest success, promoting concerts for Lynyrd Skynyrd, Charlie Daniels, Deodata, and other acts.

We found ourselves having an issue doing a concert on the Kent campus. One of our groups had a very restrictive backstage security rule in their contract rider, which if that rider was ever released would have set off a firestorm on the campus. If the contract rider was breached, then legally the band could keep the payment made to them for the show and leave, due to the contract security and safety issues set forth in the rider.

Keep in mind, the students on campus did not want to attend a concert and get hassled by uniformed police. The atmosphere was just that strong against the police, given the fact that the students were constantly rousted after having the National Guard open fire on them.

Our young concert company had an issue: How do we successfully provide concert security for this group, avoid antagonizing the Kent students and at the same time honor a contract rider that contained highly offensive provisions and prevent the group from canceling its contract due to a breach on our part as far as security is concerned?

With the help of my brother Ken Jursinski, who enrolled at Kent under the G.I. Bill, and like myself, was in the criminal justice pre-law program, we came up with the idea of a T-shirt security company composed of a number of our friends. We would keep the peace but we were not armed. We kept the rider provision confidential and secured the backstage and stage area. We did have to kick ass on occasion but that was part of the security gig. Great idea.

That concept caught on and we began doing concert security in Kent, Akron and Cleveland for major concerts put on by Belkin Productions and other major concert producers, including our own concert company, America Concerts, Inc.

We recruited the guys for our T-shirt security company who had to be able to get physical when necessary, but also use their heads in controlling a crowd of mainly college-aged students. Our guys were all ex-college football players like myself, who for whatever reason were not on college teams but still loved to play the game.

We not only ran a great T-shirt security company, but many of the guys in the company were also my teammates on our intramural flag football teams. Our team, sponsored by the bar "The Deck" with the team name "Hot Knives," went undefeated and won the Kent State school championship for flag football. The year before Ron Deem and I were on another team, sponsored by the bar "Ron-de-Vous" and that team won the independent division for the Kent State school championship for flag football. We dominated intramural flag football at Kent those two years.

As we sat there that evening reminiscing, we recalled that our T-shirt security company, Sunrise Security, was so successful that we handled the security for major headline shows like the Rolling Stones at Cleveland Municipal Stadium as well as Doobie Brothers and Crosby Stills, Nash and Young shows at Rich Stadium in Buffalo, New York.

Those shows were packed with over 100,000 people, the security controlled by only a few dozen ex-jocks with no weapons or back up, only each other to maintain the peace.

One of our security team members, Bob Bender, went on to be the personal bodyguard of Mick Jagger and was featured in a Rolling Stone article titled "Looking for Mr. Goodbar" for his prowess at concert security, which he learned while working in our company. Bender was also a key player on our flag football team guarding the middle of the line as part of our school championship team.

By the way, Bender played for the "Hot Knives" since he left the Kent team after becoming disgruntled when he thought he should be the starting linebacker instead of future NFL Hall of Famer Jack Lambert.

That is a strong ego. But we all had egos and never-lose attitudes.

George stayed in the music industry and became a great success promoting records and managing a number of acts while his wife Gloria had a successful career in her own business. My interest was in reviewing the concert contracts. I enjoyed that aspect of the business and realized my calling would ultimately be in law.

As my friends and I reminisced and tried not to get caught up in our glory days, it hit me that my life experiences at Kent State and the anti-war protests and speeches may never have been quite what they were had Kennedy not been assassinated. That great feeling of reminiscing that night immediately stopped when I considered what I just heard and my mind flashed back to my interview with Helmich at the federal prison and the stunning information he shared tying him in with the conspiracy to assassinate Kennedy.

As we talked that evening, I also recalled being backstage doing security at the Crosby, Still, Nash and Young show in Buffalo the summer of 1974. That concert was attended by more than 100,000 people. During the show, I ultimately made my way to just below the front of the stage when CSN&Y did their encore of the haunting ballad "Ohio" decrying the death of our fellow Kent State students who were shot on campus protesting the Viet Nam War that Johnson had advanced and Kennedy had vowed to avoid. I was mesmerized by the lyrics of "Ohio" as I stood in front of the stage that day taking it all in and recognizing the significant era we were in and our time in history at Kent State.

I caught myself pausing as I sat there thinking about that moment listening to "Ohio." My friends saw a blank stare on my face while I flashed back to that scene.

They asked me if I was all right.

I told them I was fine, shrugged it off and said that I was just a little tired from the long ride that day. But I could not escape what I had been told. I did not disclose to my friends in any detail as to my interview with Helmich. It would not be fair to dump on them what I had just experienced. I thought that I would ultimately provide that information to them in the future.

I assumed that within weeks or months, I would be able to release all this information into the hands of a publisher or producer to reveal the information that I learned, get Helmich's story out to the world and share the information about Helmich's indirect involvement with the Kennedy Assassination.

That was the plan until it wasn't.

That big reveal would never happen. The Federal Department of Justice would soon have me as its target.

I would soon find out that I would not be able to disclose any of the information under penalty of threatened federal prosecution. I did not know it at the time sitting there in my friends' living room in Marietta, Ga., but I would need to keep all this information secret for more than 40 years.

CHAPTER 8

Cease And Desist

DOJ LETTER BLOCKS MANUSCRIPT'S RELEASE TO THE WORLD

Joseph Helmich was smart, analytical and had a grasp of world events. In his *KAK: Manuscript*, he identified places, dates, times and events down to the last detail. He recalled the vehicle he was in, the street he was on and the methods of his spy drops. He even remembered the meal and the type of wine that he had with the Soviets during his meeting in Paris.

Helmich also was meticulous and detailed. He recalled specific conversations and directions he was given to carry out his mission, which was the direct result of spycraft training he received from his CIA handler in planning the background story to present to the Soviets.

The timing for the event was impeccable. Helmich had an amazing memory and recall, certainly reflecting on his IQ.

However, Helmich readily admitted to me and as set forth in his manuscript, he could not have carried out all of these elaborate plans over the better part of a year without spycraft training.

After I returned to Fort Myers, I shared my experience interviewing Helmich with Darlene. I not only told her what I had learned from my interview with Helmich but that he entrusted me with his manuscript. I read the manuscript in full as did Darlene. We were both stunned at what we read in context of what I had learned in my interview with Helmich in Talladega.

Reading the manuscript was chilling. I had a renewed adrenaline rush regarding this methodical plan for Joe Helmich to surrender our top-secret information to the Soviet Union to enable them to decode all our classified military messages the very day Kennedy was assassinated.

How did this information never make it into any of the Congressional hearings or the follow-up investigations to the Kennedy Assassination? No one saw this? No one connected the dots? It was not speculation. Helmich was convicted of transferring top military secrets to the Soviets on November 22, 1963. It was a highly publicized Federal trial on the front page of *The New York Times* and covered by every major U.S. newspaper. This evidence was hidden in plain sight.

In reading the manuscript, Helmich also related to his CIA involvement in Mexico and the murder of a CIA operative while he was there. The manuscript tracks Helmich's tour of duty in Viet Nam, which involved the CIA as part of the Golden Triangle drug smuggling operation. Helmich's cellmate at Talladega was Charlie Long who had referred me to Helmich. After reading the manuscript as to the events in Viet Nam, I laughed at the thought of these cellmates swapping some interesting stories about drug smuggling from their past.

After digesting the revelations in the manuscript, I formulated an approach to contact national publishers and some literary agents to determine their interest in the *KAK: Manuscript*. Based upon their responses, we tailored our approach while we considered self publishing this work. That was the plan.

From the time I left FCI Talladega, it only took a few weeks before I realized the consequences of the documents that Helmich entrusted to me.

I personally became the target of the FBI and the Department of Justice (DOJ) as the custodian of the manuscript.

Remember, the DOJ, CIA and FBI asserted that Helmich was not involved with the CIA but rather worked directly for the Soviets. They were adamant Helmich was a lone-wolf actor working for himself and sold military secrets directly to the Soviets for profit motivated by only his own self-interest. They did not accept his claim that the CIA recruited him to do this work.

Within a week or so after sending our letters to national publishing houses, the DOJ served me with a cease-and-desist letter at my law firm. This letter asserted that any release of Helmich's information could be a violation of the then recently passed *Identities Protection Act of 1982*, which made it a federal crime to release the names or identities of CIA personnel.

That letter jolted me.

I met with attorney Dennis Rehak, who initially referred me to Helmich through the Charlie Long family.

Also at this time and during our business phone conversations, attorney Rehak and I both experienced numerous odd sounds on our law office phone lines. We both compared notes and considered whether we were paranoid. I told Darlene about the situation and she came to the office and heard for herself what I had been describing. We all concluded, after also having a law office staff member identify the odd sounds, that it appeared as though our phones were being bugged.

It was a standing joke for a while that our house phone was also being tapped. I recall Darlene speaking with her mom one evening when she commented to Darlene that there were odd sounds on the phone and Darlene nonchalantly stated, "We have someone listening in on our call so keep that in mind as we talk."

We also had our concerns raised when the client file on Helmich went missing, never to be found. It did not contain much other than the DOJ letter and some correspondence to book publishers. The original *KAK: Manuscript* was stored safely off premises, and copies were strategically placed in various safe deposit boxes.

We spoke with other legal counsel to consider my duties and obligations both as a licensed attorney in Florida but also as a citizen who the DOJ had on its radar with a threat to prosecute any action on my part to release this information.

The severe criminal penalties included fines and federal imprisonment. I considered what action the U.S. Government could take against me if the names in the book - even if Helmich told me he changed them - were disclosed. With the newly passed legislation, in what context would the U.S. Government address any action on my part to release the *KAK: Manuscript*?

We discussed the severity of the law. Given the recent passage of the *Intelligence Identities Protection Act of 1982*, we had no case law or precedent to provide guidance. We also discussed that the DOJ had warned to cease and desist so further efforts also could be seen as defying the cease-and-desist directive, perhaps establishing mens rea (criminal intent). I also flashed back at being in a federal prison like Talladega — this time not visiting with an afternoon pass but as full-time resident.

I considered the DOJ's letter to me and the legal advice I received. The consensus was that I could not disclose any information that Helmich gave me, since that information, if it contained the names of CIA personnel or could lead to the identities of CIA personnel, would subject me to federal charges under the *Identities Protections Act*. The federal law put in place sealed any information that could be released.

The DOJ letter sealed my lips and blocked release of the manuscript, just as the threat of killing Joe's wife and son sealed his ability to go on the stand and protect himself.

The DOJ letter for me further raised the question that if Helmich was not involved with the CIA as an operative or recruit and was a lone-wolf traitor who leaked military secrets to the Soviets, how would he have the names of CIA personnel to disclose if he never worked with them?

And why would the DOJ have threatened me with federal prosecution for releasing the names of CIA operatives if Helmich worked only for the Soviets and was not a tool of CIA handlers? Or in any way involved with the CIA?

I spoke to my wife Darlene about this and the effect this could have on our lives. We had two young daughters, ages 5 and 2, to consider. Also, the DOJ has unlimited resources. Based upon advice by legal counsel and the uncertainty involved, I could not afford to jeopardize my family, my legal career, or of course, be exposed to federal prosecution.

If I chose to take action, which contravened the cease-and-desist letter, then I could be the target of a federal lawsuit. Even if we prevailed, court costs could bankrupt me. Even worse, if we lost, I would be convicted of a felony and face the loss of my law license and a federal prison sentence.

Regrettably, the DOJ cease-and-desist letter meant I would have to stand down and live with this secret until the FBI declassified the Helmich file.

There was no option to "Play to Win." Or "Refuse to Lose." Instead of "Never Give Up," I had to surrender, at least for the time being. Hard to take knowing what I knew.

I took the position that this cease-and-desist order was not a loss, but rather a setback for a period of time, after which we would be able to release the manuscript. It was not lost on me that the same government agencies that controlled and directed Helmich were now controlling my own activities and my ability to release the truth.

I advised Helmich of the situation. He recognized the circumstances, understood, and indicated that when the time was right, I should act, but only when the time was right. He was disappointed but he recognized that I had to bend the knee to the DOJ and give up, just as he had to accept a plea without being able to present his defense. The DOJ was one bully that unfortunately I could not stand up to.

I promised him that I would safeguard his words he wrote in his *KAK: Manuscript*. I have kept that promise.

Years later a friend of mine and retired Secret Service agent who spent eight years on Presidential Detail before he went into private contracting doing black ops missions met with me to go over the details of this book. He gave me some great insights into the information that I had learned from Helmich and a perspective that

I had not considered.

For example, when I told him of the very odd, ongoing noticeable sounds on our telephone line and our suspicions of being under surveillance, he told me something I had not thought of: That these sounds were intentional. He explained that intelligence officers listening to our phone calls in the early 1980s had sophisticated equipment and their surveillance would have gone undetected. He told me we heard the sounds because the people surveilling us wanted us to hear the sounds to send a message that we were being watched and listened to.

From time to time, I have been reminded of reports that came out of new Kennedy Assassination evidence. Others had the courage to step forward. Some risked their jobs and others their reputation to advance the evidence that they had. Others made documentaries or movies, knowing that they would get criticism as being a conspiracy theorist. Yet those people had the courage to pursue what they believed to be true.

While I have carved out a successful legal career, it has haunted me that I could not take steps to release this information and be as forthcoming as others who risked their reputation and fortune to reveal information that they had.

Many did so to expose the truth behind the assassination. Each year more of that truth has come out. I also thought that if others had the information in the *KAK: Manuscript,* that this additional information might support their inquiries and perhaps lead to more information being released on the Kennedy Assassination.

I had to comfort myself that the imposed silence was the best approach since I still couldn't compromise my family or myself or be exposed to a claim that I violated the *Identities Protection Act.* I tried to justify it as a delay rather than an absolute prohibition. I didn't have the courage that was shown by those others who did step forward and risked attacks on themselves and their reputations. I assured myself and held onto the belief that someday I would be able to release this information, perhaps to wash away the guilt I felt in not getting this story out.

From late 1982 until now, I guarded this information and did not attempt to publish the contents of what Helmich provided me. I thought that eventually I would be able to release the information after months or a few years.

However, I have had to guard this critical story with me for more than 40 years since that is how long it took for the Helmich file to be declassified and then for his widow Jean to authorize the release of the manuscript.

Every time I saw a documentary or read about the Kennedy Assassination, my impactful interview with Hemich became fresh in my mind. As did the writings of Helmich in his manuscript. I would occasionally re-read his manuscript. Due to the DOJ notice, I was helpless to do anything with the manuscript. I did not have the courage to release the manuscript for fear of reprisal from the DOJ. I hated that feeling.

The FBI finally declassified their file on the Joseph G. Helmich investigation, dubbed *Operation Hook Shot.*

The declassified - if you want to call it that - file contains heavily redacted information. Page after page contain blackouts. The FBI, after 40 years, still refused to publish specific items that Helmich provided to them in those nine interviews. What do they want to keep from the American public?

Why does the U.S. Government act as though it is Col. Jessup and we are all Lieutenant Kaffees? We all know the truth or at least know that Kennedy's murder was not as described in the Warren Report. We knew that Oswald was not a lone-wolf actor but rather a patsy caught up in this larger plan. He was murdered to forever silence him and his involvement.

On Feb. 12, 2025, U.S. Rep. Anna Paulina Luna, who is heading a Task Force on the Declassification of Federal Secrets, said she believed "two shooters" were involved in the assassination of JFK while speaking during a Capitol Hill press conference. She added the American people have been "treated like children for too long and kept in the dark by those we elected to serve us."

CHAPTER 9

Digging For Answers

ROADBLOCKS ENCOUNTERED
IN SEARCH FOR THE TRUTH

I obtained a full copy of the declassified FBI *Operation Hook Shot* file kept on Helmich to begin review and analysis. I did several Freedom of Information Act requests on Helmich as well as on the Kennedy Assassination.

As part of the information obtained, I secured a copy of the famous *Playboy* article with the interview of Jim Garrison on the Kennedy Assassination. The article ignited national conspiracy feelings. The article was the precursor for the trial in New Orleans conducted by Garrison. That investigation and the trial was eventually made into a poignant film by Oliver Stone called *JFK*. Released in 1991, Stone updated the *JFK* film by releasing *JFK Revisited: Through the Looking Glass*, in 2021.

Thirty years after the first film exposed many issues in the Kennedy Assassination, we continue to have more questions than answers. Each year the more we find out, the more we are convinced that this was a well-thought-out plan by a select few to take over control of the U.S. Government.

The Warren Commission's report on the Kennedy Assassination has been questioned and criticized since many have found its findings illogical. Significant evidence that was available was disregarded, key evidence was apparently altered or manipulated, key witnesses were ignored, or their testimonies changed.

The Warren Commission theory of the assassination was never accepted by the majority of Americans who saw it for what it was: The U.S. Government covered up the facts or manipulated the truth.

What I saw and what many others observed was that the Warren Commission was selectively following leads that supported their predetermined theory, shaping the evidence when the true facts were apparent and in plain sight.

Most saw the Warren Commission as intentionally not investigating crucial information. Rather it started its investigation with a foregone conclusion of a lone-wolf gunman. With that prejudgment in mind, they began assembling information to support their prejudgment. A fatally flawed investigation.

The Warren Commission failed, intentionally or otherwise, to connect the dots. Wouldn't it be worth investigating a trial transcript of a warrant officer who claimed to turn over top-secret materials to the Soviets in the fall of 1963; and that he was commanded to do so before Nov. 22, 1963? Of course it would, unless that did not fit neatly into the Warren Commission's judgment made in advance of all of the evidence being identified and evaluated.

FBI Agent James K. Murphy led the investigation into Helmich's activities and testified at Helmich's trial. In the 126 pages of testimony, he confirmed what Helmich and his wife Jean both have stated: that Helmich and Jean traveled to Paris around the time of the assassination as part of his espionage activities. He specifically said:

"... during the meeting that I had with him on Feb. 4 (1981), he told me that he believed his wife accompanied him twice to Paris, one time with his sister, Margie Ann, and the second time by himself, but he talked to his wife last night or the evening of Feb. 4, and she refreshed his memory and stated that she only traveled back to Paris with him once, which would have been around the time of President Kennedy's assassination, so he wanted to make that clarification." [9-1]

Yet at the trial, the next question was not to inquire of this significant coincidence of the travel being "around Nov. 22, 1963." There was no follow up on the coincidental dates nor if this was connected to the Soviets. Nothing.

Rather, the testimony simply drifted off into what Helmich did with the money that he received on that trip. Absolutely no follow-up questions by the Prosecution team on the significance of Helmich and his wife being on a pre-arranged flight to Paris the day of the Kennedy Assassination and receiving $131,000 for surrendering the then-current key codes on the day of the assassination.

What a missed opportunity. Or was it? Perhaps the Prosecution did not want to open up the door on this evidence and therefore kept that fact low-key.

Helmich's indictment and conviction was overlooked as it related to the timing of the espionage act on Nov. 22, 1963. Someone knew, whether it was the Soviets, the CIA or others. However, it became another piece of evidence that was disregarded or covered up.

Why is it more than 60 years after the assassination and the U.S. Government still refuses to release all the classified information on the assassination with no redactions? Again, what does it want to keep from us?

I am not a conspiracy theorist. As an attorney I review facts and evidence and identify what I believe to be the logical conclusion to the evidence presented, using my legal training and in part utilizing the principle of the Occam's razor problem solving approach.

Essentially, Occam's razor theory is that the simplest explanation pointing to a result is generally the best one to select. Unnecessary or extraneous assumptions introduce uncertainties which exposes the process to errors. Occam's razor analysis is based upon the probability theory that fundamentally by introducing numerous assumptions to a problem, such effort inherently introduces the greater possibility of error. If an assumption does not improve the accuracy of a theory, its only effect is to increase the probability that the overall theory is incorrect and should not be considered a key assumption due to the chance for introducing an error to the process.

That by using the approach that the Warren Commission used, which was extraneous assumptions to prove that there was only one shooter, simply results in the analysis containing numerous odd assumptions and increasing the possibility of errors in the results.

The best example of introducing numerous improper assumptions is in the Warren Report into the Kennedy Assassination by the contrived Single Bullet Theory. The Single Bullet Theory advanced goes something like this:

> *"With a single shot from Oswald's rifle, a 6.5-millimeter bullet pierced Kennedy's suit coat from the rear before puncturing his body to the right of his spine. The bullet exited Kennedy's body through the front of his neck below his Adam's apple.*
>
> *The bullet — later dubbed Commission Exhibit 399, or CE 399 — then punctured Connally's back, shattering his fifth right rib bone. After exiting the front of Connally's chest, the bullet shot through his right wrist, breaking one of his wrist bones, before burying itself beneath the skin of Connally's left thigh*
>
> *This path of travel — considered highly unlikely by critics of the single bullet theory — means CE 399 went through the bodies of two adult men, tore through about 15 inches of human flesh, broke two bones and punctured 15 different layers of clothing. The bullet was recovered at Parkland Memorial Hospital on a gurney in the hospital corridor. It was later determined that the gurney was next to the one that carried Connally into the hospital."*

Apply Occam's razor analysis to this wild assumption the Warren Commission passed off onto the American public as true: introducing numerous assumptions created a greater possibility of error. If an assumption does not improve the accuracy of a theory, its only effect is to increase the probability that the overall theory is incorrect. Here multiple upon multiple unsupported assumptions leading to a pristine bullet purportedly found resting on the gurney at the hospital, unbelievably being passed off as falling out of Gov. Connolly's leg is explained away with the Single Bullet Theory. The Warren Commission sold that story to the American public with a straight face. The majority of Americans know that they were lied to.

The Single Bullet Theory had to be contrived to advance the conclusion made by the Warren Commission that Oswald acted alone. If the Single Bullet Theory is not accepted, then every conclusion in the Warren Report falls apart. Without the Single Bullet Theory, the only explanation is that there was more than one gunman that day in Dallas. More than one gunman means there was a conspiracy. More than one gunman means that someone or some group knew and planned the event well in advance. That would not fit in with the Warren Commission's pre-judgment of what took place: A lone-wolf gunman was the only one responsible.

The entry wound to the front of the head had to be altered. The autopsy could not be performed by a well-trained doctor in these matters in Dallas. Rather the autopsy was performed by doctors who had no experience in doing gunshot autopsies. Evidence was altered or evidence was created to support a fatally flawed theory of a single gunman performing the act.

Does anyone who has ever fired a weapon and retrieved a spent bullet after it hit a target believe that Single Bullet Theory is plausible and that there would be a pristine bullet laying on a gurney as the one the Warren Commission claimed? Of course not. The Single Bullet Theory violates every tenet of Occam's razor analysis.

Parts of the Warren Commission Report on the Single Bullet Theory could have been written by Joseph Goebbels. He has been credited with saying the bigger the lie, the more people will believe it.

I applied Occam's razor analysis to the unrefuted facts involving Helmich and for which he was convicted: Helmich was notified well in advance of Nov. 22, 1963, to be on a plane to Paris to deliver top-secret information to the Soviets. Logically that means someone knew and planned for an event to take place that day. The fact that Helmich, along with his wife Jean, boarded that plane and then

Helmich ultimately delivered the top-secret information to the Soviets, again by the application of the Occam's razor analysis, leads to the conclusion that a group of people knew in advance what was to take place on Nov. 22, 1963.

Following that logic and application of Occam's razor analysis leads to the conclusion that the Soviets were provided with access to top military communications to be assured that the U.S. would not be retaliating against the Soviets.

As an attorney, an argument as to the undisputed facts involving Helmich's activities could have been presented to the Trier of Fact and in my opinion would have a far better chance of being accepted as true than the wildly exotic and implausible Single Bullet Theory that was peddled to the American public.

In the Helmich trial, the goal would have been to only place reasonable doubt in at least one juror and Helmich's story could do that. The Warren Commission sold the highly improbable, and I suggest impossible tale of the Single Bullet Theory. I believe a jury could have accepted Helmich's explanation and perhaps even granted him an acquittal. He was never allowed to present his defense.

With that background in mind, we started our research into the matter and began reviewing documents and making requests surrounding Helmich's activities and conduct.

Unearthing The Trial Transcript

I contacted and interviewed Helmich's initial defense counsel, Peter Dearing, who was court appointed to represent Helmich in the federal trial. In my interview with Dearing, he related to me that Helmich cooperated with the FBI in numerous interviews and his statements to them about his activities were directly admissible. This severely compromised Helmich's case and gave the prosecution numerous statements admissible against Helmich at trial.

Yet the affidavit of Jean Helmich indicated that the FBI threatened Helmich and coerced the information that he provided over a series of nine separate interviews.

These facts also supported the position Helmich did not hide anything. He believed that when he disclosed that he worked with the CIA, his activities and assignment would be recognized and that his actions would be done for a purpose as his CIA handler ordered. However, the CIA did not step in once he was charged with espionage. Helmich realized that he was abandoned and left hanging out there. He then had to be silenced, first by death threats to his wife and child, then indirectly by the passage of *the Identities Protection Act* of 1982.

Once the FBI declassified Helmich's file, we began assembling background information and doing our research which also included a request for a copy of the entire Federal Court case file. When he pled guilty, the case file was closed. And amazingly to me, there was no file record of the formal trial proceedings at the Federal Court house. No hard copy. No microfilm. No microfiche.

I referenced and reviewed the Guide to Judiciary Policy, Volume 10 Public Access and Records. Chapter: Records Management.

This is the formal federal government directives on how court files are handled and stored.

There is a retention period specified for case files and also a special designation for files designated for historical value, which are designated "Permanent" in the schedules.

The schedule indicates in Schedule 2 the following: "Any criminal case file determined by court officials or the National Archives and Records Administration (NARA) to have historical value. Permanent. Transfer records to NARA 15 years after the close of the case." 9-2

I assumed that one of the most high-profile federal jury trials on Soviet espionage would be considered within the definition of: "Any criminal case file determined by court officials or NARA to have historical value."

We made numerous formal requests to the Clerk of the Federal Court in Jacksonville, the DOJ, the defense trial attorney or anyone else involved in the Helmich trial to help locate the actual federal court case file, on microfilm or otherwise. We secured a copy of the docket but the actual court filings are all missing. Along with any transcripts or the Judge's trial notes, motions, pleadings, trial transcripts, etc.

After numerous requests of the Federal Clerk of Courts and FOIA requests as well as requests to the law firm involved in representing Helmich the result had been the same: the complete court case file is missing and was nowhere to be found. Other than the docket sheet, the more than 1,000 pages of this high-profile criminal case had disappeared.

I am generally familiar with federal criminal case files. Although I am not a criminal attorney, I have acted as the only expert witness testifying on behalf of the defendant in a Federal Court case involving criminal fraud prosecuted by the U.S. Attorney and supported by the FBI's investigation.

In that Federal criminal case in the Federal Court in the Southern District of Florida, I reviewed hundreds of pages of trial information and the entire FBI and DOJ file against the defendant for whom I prepared my testimony.

My testimony, along with the great defense team, defeated the FBI and DOJ in the case of United States of America vs. Eve Rosen. On April 22, 2011, the accused, Attorney Eve Rosen, was acquitted on all 13 felony counts for which she was charged. I was happy for my client and her defense team. I enjoyed the victory over the DOJ and the FBI. The point being there is a massive amount of trial material that should have been stored on the Helmich file. There was no trial information on the Helmich file that the U.S. Government would produce.

The evidence of the Helmich trial that I wanted to review, fundamentally the entire case file, is like all the other evidence and witness information in any way touching on the Kennedy Assassination: the evidence either goes missing, is redacted, destroyed, buried somewhere or ultimately lost in the dustbin of history. Or as better stated in the famous book *1984* as applied to the evidence surrounding the Kennedy Assassination:

"Everything faded into the mist. The past was erased, the erasure was forgotten, the lie became truth," wrote George Orwell in *1984*.

Ultimately after repeated requests of the Federal Clerk and FOIA requests with no success, we hired Don Corbett, a great private investigator. Don is a retired detective with 40 years of experience. He previously worked cold-case homicide investigations in Youngstown, Ohio, a notorious mob-influenced town well known for murders-for-hire. A cold-case murder detective sounded like just the guy to look into this file involving the most high-profile murder of the century.

It took Don a year to come up with the information we sought. Every time he called, he needed to give his credentials.

While some call takers or government contractors didn't want to help, others didn't know how to help. Don said many were overwhelmed. He also said some may have avoided helping because of the sensitivity of the documents.

Don just kept digging and digging. Eventually he found the right people to help. The "hidden" files that seemed to be missing in action ultimately were moved from Federal Court in Jacksonville to a pigeon hole in the bowels of the National Archives in a Georgia facility. The national archives warehouse in Atlanta has rows and rows of files. Think of one of the final scenes in Indiana Jones' *Raiders of the Lost Ark*.

Using Accession Number: 021870060 and Federal Archives Location number 11096091, those were the keys that finally unlocked the door. Don located the entire file, if you can believe it, just when it seemed like the entire Federal court system could not locate a single page of the trial transcript or had any idea of where to search.

We now have the entire trial file with all of the information requests consisting of more than 1,000 pages of trial material including the transcripts of trial testimony of Four-Star General William Westmoreland and Three-Star General Thomas Rienzi, both of whom personally appeared and testified at Helmich's trial as to the significance of the top-secret coding equipment and crypto codes Helmich sold to the Soviets in Paris in the Fall of 1963.

Joseph G. Helmich ultimately died in prison in 2002 having a massive heart attack after suffering from mouth and throat cancer, unable to speak and dying before his file was declassified. Certainly, before any of this information in his manuscript could be revealed to the public without fear of prosecution from the DOJ and without direct ratification from Joseph Helmich other than through his manuscript.

Helmich was interviewed on CBS by Charlie Rose in a 1985 documentary piece titled, "The Spies Among Us," in which Helmich talked of being taught spycraft by a CIA handler.

In the court file, the U.S. Government indicated that Helmich was taught spycraft and training from the Soviets. As intelligent as he was, Helmich had a great deal of assistance in planning and executing one of the largest turnovers of military secrets occurring in the Fall of 1963 and culminating, per Helmich, on the day Kennedy was assassinated. Hard to refute that position as the U.S. Government asserted and convicted him for that act of espionage.

Helmich spent the rest of his life in prison in part for what he did on Nov. 22, 1963, which was to surrender the key codes to U.S. Military communications. This enabled the Soviets to know that America would not retaliate against the Soviet Union. No justification for that action.

Yet no one could connect these dots? How was that possible? This information was hidden in plain sight.

After the declassification of *Operation Hook Shot* occurred and while I began reassembling information on this matter, I had to locate Helmich's widow, Jean, to determine what her wishes were as to the manuscript and the release of Joe's story.

I had never spoken to her before. I had no idea where she lived. I would try to find her, convinced she would be excited when I explained to her what I had discovered and what I was prepared to do.

9-1: Page 88, lines 3-10 of trial testimony of FBI agent James K. Murphy, Sept. 25, 1981.

9-2: Guide to Judiciary Policy, Volume 10, Public Access and Records. Chapter: Records Management: N1-021-11-1, Item 6c

CHAPTER 10

Recruited For Assignment

SPYCRAFT KNOWLEDGE SUGGESTS CIA INVOLVEMENT

In court proceedings that I finally reviewed, the U.S. Attorney scoffed at Helmich's claim he was recruited to perform these espionage activities.

That is what Helmich told the FBI in his nine interviews.

Helmich explained every assignment, which included selling the Soviets the U.S. Government's key codes for use directly after the Kennedy Assassination; witnessing the murder of a CIA operative in Mexico; and being involved with the heroin drug smuggling operation that the CIA handled while he was in Viet Nam. Helmich detailed all of this with specificity.

Helmich readily admitted many times over that he would not have had the expertise to pull this off without significant training by his handlers. Apparently, none of this mattered to the FBI. Either that, or the bureau had been directed not to open up the topic. No explanation as to how Helmich was intensely trained to engage in sophisticated spycraft or by whom. The missions he carried out took expertise and the exercise of serious spycraft.

So, the news reports on the trial never provided the public with the information Helmich intended to demonstrate. He never took the stand and his side of the story was buried.

Helmich told me during our interview that when the FBI first approached him while managing a hardware store in Buffalo, New York, an agent manhandled him in the stock room at the rear of the store and stuck a gun down his throat demanding that he provide answers.

"You take it seriously when an FBI agent puts his pistol down your throat and demands answers," Helmich said in an eerily calm and controlled manner, as if the recollection for him was just part of the job description.

It's hardly the methodical FBI approach if it truly had information on Helmich, rather more like desperation after 17 years of investigations with nothing to show for it.

I had to challenge Helmich on some of his statements.

I could not accept them just because he said they were true. Clearly however, the newspaper articles were not the whole story and were slanted to paint Helmich as an uneducated traitor who was broken by the FBI.

Even the U.S. Government in the trial proceedings knew that was not true. As Helmich's well-credentialed defense counsel, Peter Dearing, pointed out at trial, the FBI and the Prosecution had no evidence whatsoever on Helmich's conduct other than what Helmich provided them and upon which it built its case.

That was part of the Defense's position in the sentencing phase of the case to remind the Court as well as the government that Helmich fully cooperated and provided them with evidence of his conduct.

That fact was inconvenient for prosecutors, whose goal was to get a conviction and not the full truth of what happened.

Keep it simple: lone-wolf traitor acting on his own.

The news article reflected that U.S. Government storyline.

If the full truth was exposed, a jury might form reasonable doubt on Helmich's actions.

Was he ordered to do so?

The jury might also want to know the basis for the timing of the pre-planned espionage event in Paris in the days immediately after Nov. 22, 1963.

Clandestine Activities Ignored By Media

Helmich said he voluntarily shared with the FBI his involvement with the Soviets in Paris in 1963 and his other assignments in Mexico City and Viet Nam through his CIA handlers. Helmich provided names, dates and explicit details on all of his activities.

The Prosecution in the Court proceedings acknowledged Helmich's clandestine activities in Viet Nam but never pressed this point. U.S. Attorney Gary Betz even conceded this in Court documents:

"... One can only look at his contact in 1964 by remembering the testimony at the trial. In July 1964, he was assigned to an (Army Security Agency) outfit in Viet Nam, and he had orders to go there. ... Mr. Helmich knew that he was going to a very secretive outfit in Viet Nam." [10-1]

To put this in context of what Helmich advised the FBI, wrote in his manuscript and was included in the trial transcript: He was assigned to the Army Security Agency in Viet Nam. The ASA was the Army's signal intelligence branch.

ASA was primarily responsible for intercepting and analyzing enemy radio communications.

Most of its units focused upon signal intelligence but most, if not all of its units contained human intelligence specialists, as well as interrogators and counter-intelligence specialists.

The official ASA motto was "Semper Vigiles - Always Vigilant" but its better known motto was "In God we trust; all others we monitor." That reflected its clandestine mission of monitoring enemy signals.

ASA personnel often deployed deep within enemy territory. During Viet Nam, personnel posed as military advisors to South Vietnamese forces while secretly monitoring enemy communications.

Viet Nam ended in 1975. The ASA, which began in 1945, merged two years later with the U.S. Army's Military Intelligence component to create the United States Army Intelligence and Security Command (INSCOM).

Helmich's assignment highlighted and supported the proposition he was a CIA operative. If the U.S. Government red-flagged and investigated him, why not just put him on a desk job until the investigation ended? Why send him to an organization that monitored and worked in counterintelligence during the ramp up of the Viet Nam War?

It is not logical unless he was affiliated with the CIA and it wanted him to assist in clandestine affairs.

Helmich detailed in his manuscript that his CIA handlers gave him directions to work with ASA intelligence units on counterintelligence, including a psychological operation (psy-ops) in Viet Nam on captured North Viet Nam soldiers. The CIA ran the ASA unit that he was assigned. Of course, why would the Prosecution bring up that additional inconvenient fact?

Helmich told me of his involvement with the CIA in the drug smuggling operation in the Golden Triangle - a mountainous region in Myanmar, Thailand and Laos, where opium and heroin were produced and trafficked. He also said he was part of a plot where the CIA planned to murder him and some of his team members in Saigon over a dispute as to the release of a CIA heroin stash.

Helmich also identified other missions that he was assigned to perform in Mexico City. He watched the CIA run drug smuggling activities such as the Air America campaign. Air America was an American passenger and cargo airline established in 1946 and covertly owned and operated by the CIA from 1950 to 1976. This campaign was run to fund clandestine CIA activities. Helmich described the storage of the duffel bags full of heroin and his affiliation with the Quartermaster operations in Saigon during his tour of duty in Viet Nam.

Yet with this supposed ongoing serious investigation into him as a possible security threat or worse, we are to accept that the army assigned him to highly sensitive intelligence operations in Viet Nam? And his assignment was to a CIA-run ASA unit doing counterintelligence for a buildup on the most significant conflict the United States engaged in since the Korean War?

Would logical deduction not suggest that the CIA worked with ASA's intelligence units on counterintelligence as Helmich indicated and that he also was actively involved in CIA activities in Viet Nam? And this assignment was arranged to place Helmich in a sensitive position to engage in counterintelligence?

Or was this just another coincidence?

That a soldier under investigation is given a top-secret assignment important in the buildup of Viet Nam as America's next big war? Does that make sense?

The Times article also did not report on Helmich's activities in Mexico City, which he said was part of his CIA operations. In the trial transcript, the Prosecution confirmed Helmich was paid an additional $30,000 (equivalent to more than $300,000 in 2025) for his activities in Mexico City: "After this, in July, 1964, there was a trip to Mexico for $30,000. At the time he was under orders to this outfit," said Gary Betz, U.S. Attorney for the Dept of Justice. [10-2]

"The outfit" U.S. Attorney Betz seemed to reference was the Soviets. Helmich indicated that the "outfit" was actually the CIA. In either event, the large payment for his work in Mexico City and Viet Nam seems significant to me. The timing under the circumstances as well as his assignment raised a number of red flags overlooked by the FBI and the Prosecution.

Dire Straits Backstory Doesn't Add Up

The New York Times storyline was that Helmich bounced a few checks and he was desperate, so he went rogue and turned over the U.S. Army's top-secret coding equipment to the Soviets in the Fall of 1963 to save his ass. The story being sold is this desperate, uneducated individual performed these major espionage acts as his only way to pay off some bad checks. Really?

If this full story was presented to a jury could Helmich have raised a reasonable doubt that this was an orchestrated assignment which Helmich fulfilled flawlessly?

The logic of his storyline just doesn't add up for me.

Through my educational background in Catholic High School, the study of religious philosophy and logic, and in my pre-law school college courses as well as at the private law school I attended, I learned critical thinking and inductive and deductive reasoning.

Inductive and deductive reasoning in law involves assembling specific facts, drawing conclusions from those facts, applying logic to the facts and then further applying those facts to the law. This creates a legal argument to prove a conclusion, which I do in advocating civil cases. In criminal defense, using inductive and deductive reasoning allows defense counsel to argue a defense position to raise a reasonable doubt in the jury's mind to gain an acquittal.

Perhaps oversimplified, but that is my take on logic, inductive and deductive reasoning and being a litigator and advocate for my client. It is a skill and an art. It takes work and time to master.

In law school, I learned that as an attorney, I can't actually prove that something happened or did not happen without question. Nonetheless as an effective advocate, I could establish and compile evidence that supported the legal argument I was advancing and argue that my position is undeniably true, or at least so when the preponderance of evidence standard was applied.

The preponderance of the evidence standard is what I am used to since that is applied in civil cases, whereas the more challenging beyond reasonable doubt standard is applied in criminal actions.

As a Plaintiff in a civil case, you have to prove your theory by a preponderance of the evidence.

In a criminal case, the Prosecution has to prove its case beyond a reasonable doubt. Big proof difference. So, in a criminal case, the Defense only has to have the jury determine that there is a reasonable doubt and it prevails.

In a civil case, a defendant must prove to the Trier of Fact that the Plaintiff has not proven its case by a preponderance of evidence.

I considered Helmich's arguments and what the U.S. Government advanced as its argument at the trial up to the point the Prosecution rested. At such time Helmich had a chance to explain what he did and why he did it in his own words. He would have had the commanding role of narrator as to what he voluntarily told the FBI and why in those nine separate interviews. From the start, he created the narrative.

10-1: Pages 39-40 from the Transcript of the Sentencing Hearing before the Honorable Susan H. Black, United States District Court on October 16, 1981.

10-2: Page 40 lines 11-14 from the Transcript of the Sentencing Hearing before the Honorable Susan H. Black, United States District Court on October 16, 1981.

CHAPTER 11

His Own Worst Enemy

HELMICH'S WORDS SABOTAGE HIM

In the many years since my interview with Helmich, I have wrestled with the fact that he clearly had a great opportunity to create reasonable doubt in the jury's mind as to his guilt or innocence. The U.S. Government's position rested solely on Helmich's statements to the FBI. The best person to explain those statements was Helmich. His narrative controlled the entire proceeding.

As Helmich's excellent defense attorney, Peter Dearing, stated in the case:

> *"Let me point out at this time also that we're in the totality of these proceedings, to believe Mr. Helmich, we're obliged to believe him for one reason, and that is the only evidence against him is what he has said. The Government had absolutely no other evidence to bring into a court to seek an indictment or seek a prosecution that indicated that Mr. Helmich ever compromised anything. The evidence against Mr. Helmich is his own statements."* [11-1]

While arguably Helmich's statements could cut both ways, he controlled the narrative of what he said to the FBI and why. He also could steer the jury to at least consider his position. If it did, he had a fighting chance. All he had to do was raise a reasonable doubt in the jury's mind. There was plenty of that doubt here. And plenty of critical information was never addressed by the Prosecution or the media.

What an opportunity to lay out the case for Helmich's involvement with the CIA and expose what happened behind the scenes in 1963 and the timing of just that one event. Years of espionage activity followed, which clearly can be inferred as CIA involvement in his clandestine activities in Mexico City and Viet Nam. Certainly, at a minimum, it would create reasonable doubt in the mind of even one juror that Helmich was not this one-off, lone-wolf traitor who in a panic just surrendered top military secrets to the Soviets.

However, there is a big reason Helmich pleaded guilty and accepted the plea rather than take the stand to defend himself. It was more than the fact that he had voluntarily released all the damning statements to the FBI as was recognized by his defense counsel. Helmich was fearful of the threats made upon the life of his wife and son but did not share that with his defense counsel.

Helmich's activities were orchestrated and deliberate to achieve the goals of an organization. Logically, this seemed to be much more than a series of random, unconnected acts.

With the penalty of a life sentence if convicted, why not take the opportunity to present the defense Helmich had? Why take a plea to a life sentence? The FBI knew only what Helmich told them. Nothing more. Its case rested with what Helmich told them. They were focused on a conviction for Helmich handing secrets to the Soviets in the Fall of 1963 and receiving a massive payoff.

The U.S. Government wanted a conviction on the basic charges that they thought they could prove in general. Nothing more. They had no evidence of the event. They only knew that he held a top-secret clearance designation and spent years working in such a position in various countries. They knew that the U.S. Army said he had two bad debts of $500 and $700 while in Paris.

That is all it had.

No evidence of the missing top-secret materials or equipment.

No evidence of the pay off.

No tracking of money into Helmich's bank account from the Soviets.

No corroborating witnesses.

The army had only Helmich's statements which led them to facts that they unearthed with his cooperation and then used to prosecute him. They did not dare to interject a component of the timing of the Kennedy Assassination with his espionage acts. They did not want to open that door for the jury. That would have to be advanced by the defense. The U.S. Government already had in place a plan that would prevent that from ever happening.

Helmich could have stuck a dagger in the heart of the Prosecution by his defense and his explanation of what he did and why he did it. He also could share the timing of the transfer of the top-secret information as well as who gave him orders and directions.

After reviewing the court documents, the *KAK: Manuscript* and my interview with Helmich, an acquittal was clearly in reach. Reasonable doubt could be planted as to every position asserted by the Prosecution. If Helmich took the stand and advanced his case, a jury in 1981 would have also had to consider that on Nov. 22, 1963 while the assassination of President Kennedy was occurring, Helmich was en route to Paris to complete his spy mission.

Does that not raise a reasonable doubt that this assassination was planned well in advance of the actual assassination? Helmich testimony would have eviscerated the Prosecution's position that he acted in a desperate panic.

The sophistication of the actions taken by Helmich, as he described in his manuscript and which he would have described to the jury, would have belied all of the Prosecution's positions that a lone-wolf actor in a moment of desperation surrendered top secrets to the Soviets to cover two minor debts.

The Helmich jury would have had to consider his testimony and weigh some of the undisputed facts he could have testified to, along with the intricate details of his espionage activities and methodology.

To prove criminal conspiracy, the U.S. Government needed to prove beyond a reasonable doubt that two or more people agreed to commit a crime and took a concrete step toward its completion.

The U.S. Government must also prove that the conspirators intended to break the law and knew of the plan. The FBI did not want to go there. Doing so could have meant indicting members of the CIA or other government intelligence agencies.

The Prosecution would have also had to explain that the top-secret turnover in Paris directly after the Kennedy Assassination was merely a coincidence. That had to be considered an untenable position for the Prosecution to overcome.

Why not buy the victory and seal Helmich's lips, then conveniently blame it on a lone-wolf actor? Helmich's lips would be sealed, like many of the other witnesses to the Kennedy Assassination. The U.S. Government would have its conviction.

These are observations of someone who knows the law, knows the legal way of succeeding and knows how to find a path to victory.

After interviewing Joseph Helmich and reading his manuscript, there are times when I almost wish I had defended him.

Almost.

11-1: Statement by Attorney Peter L. Dearing, counsel for Defendant Joseph George Helmich. Page 18 lines 10-18-14 from the Transcript of the Sentencing Hearing before the Honorable Susan H. Black, United States District Court on October 16, 1981.

CHAPTER 12

Reconsidering Helmich's Defense

SPY ALSO QUESTIONS WHETHER HE WAS FRAMED

As an AV rated and triple Florida Bar Board Certified attorney, I practice civil law and litigation at a high level.

It's a different legal discipline, but I do respect criminal defense counsel and the skills needed. I have made closing arguments to juries, but I have never made a closing argument to a jury in a criminal case.

However, I would have liked to have made that argument to the jurors sitting on the Helmich criminal trial and see their faces when I described where he was the day Kennedy was shot. I also would have liked to talk about all the events leading up to that day and after, including Helmich's activities in Mexico City and Viet Nam at the direction of his CIA handler.

I think another key point I would've shared was the key codes. Helmich indicated they had a short useful life that coincided with the time period directly after the Kennedy Assassination.

The Court proceedings and Helmich's *KAK: Manuscript* led me to conclude the CIA, perhaps the Soviets, recruited him to perform this significant act of espionage for the sole purpose of providing the Soviets with the codes at a critical time in U.S. history. That critical time period was the window of time directly after the Kennedy Assassination.

Again, I am in no way second guessing the well-qualified defense attorney of Helmich, Peter Dearing, a former Assistant U.S. Attorney with a high security clearance. Helmich, as the client, instructed his attorney to accept a plea deal. Defense counsel did his best to advise Helmich, but in the end, every lawyer has to follow his client's requests.

Fundamentally, a criminal defendant controls the decision whether to accept a plea bargain, not his defense counsel. It is the defendant alone that makes the final decision to accept or reject a plea offer with input and advice from defense counsel. Consider that this situation also involved a sophisticated defendant with an IQ of 147, according to *United Press International*, so he was well-informed and capably made a decision that affected the rest of his life.

Also consider Helmich never indicated to his defense counsel that the evening before he was to start his defense, he received a call at the jail from his CIA handler that indicated if he testified about his activities, his wife and son would be killed. Helmich's defense counsel did the best as to what he was instructed to do under the circumstances. Armed with all this information that Helmich kept from Dearing, it seems clear that Helmich's well-qualified defense counsel could have raised reasonable doubt to the U.S. Government's charges if he was permitted.

Helmich prevented his defense counsel from attempting to save him by putting him on the stand to tell his story to the jury. Helmich had a more important goal: Saving the life of his wife and son by accepting a plea bargain.

The cover story that he had bad debts was a contrived and well-thought-out backstory based upon the spycraft training he was provided by his CIA handler (or perhaps a Soviet mole in the CIA). This was not an act of desperation over a few bad checks.

Compare all this and match it up with the ninth-grade dropout description portrayed in *The Times* story. Would this defense not raise a reasonable doubt in the jury's mind as to his actions and how he was able to navigate all these actions without being directed to do so since although intelligent, he did not have the training in this field to carry out such an elaborate mission?

In doing my research, it was indicated that the FBI began its investigation due to an anonymous tip. After 17 years? This gave me the impression that Helmich was working under the direction of someone or some organization. For some reason it was necessary to rein him in at that time. The FBI had all of this information for 17 years and did nothing to act upon it until they received an anonymous tip? None of it added up.

Apply inductive and deductive thinking and logic and the FBI's position falls apart. And when he was approached by the FBI, Helmich chose voluntarily to debrief the FBI on all his espionage activities over months of meetings? Helmich voluntarily provided them with all of the information in which he was involved without any plea deal and clearly no immunity from prosecution. Why would he say anything without counsel unless he felt someone or some organization would step in on his behalf? He assumed that he had cover from some organization. But that did not happen.

Helmich told me he realized that he might have been set up as the patsy, characterized as a selfish traitor and threatened to confess to silence him and his activities, especially those occurring on Nov. 22, 1963. He told me that he realized that he had been taken advantage of and felt betrayed. He lamented that he might have been played in an elaborate scheme by an organization with a motive surrounding the Kennedy Assassination.

The facts still absolutely support that there was prior knowledge of the events that would occur on Kennedy's assassination and someone wanted to get access to provide top-secret intelligence and war plans directly after Nov. 22, 1963 to the Soviets.

None of the background information from *The Times* article or the other articles that I read preparing for my interview with Helmich reflected the facts I discovered. None of the information that I read made sense after discussing these events with Helmich.

The Times also produced an interview from Helmich's friends and relatives that indicated he lived a "hand-to-mouth existence." The article quoted his wife Jean, who said that the U.S. Government's storyline was, "a pack of lies."

Well said. The facts supported Jean's opinion.

Helmich had various jobs that generated an income. Yet, per the article, he was living at a poverty level? Because he bought two cars and a small house? When he was arrested, he was managing a hardware store in Buffalo. But he was financially destitute? It does not add up.

In court proceedings, Dearing asserted Helmich had only $14 to his name when the Court set his bond at $500,000. None of this made sense to me. Helmich clearly was charged with and allegedly received a massive payment for a significant handover of the highest U.S. Military secrets, but now he was at the poverty level?

My interview quickly debunked information that I had on Helmich going into the meeting at FCI Talladega.

His demeanor and the manner and method he described events contrasted with what I read.

The news stories in my opinion were disinformation or perhaps shaped news to point the reader in the direction the FBI and the DOJ wanted to advance their narratives that Helmich was just another lone individual performing a terrible act of desperation over two bad debts.

Helmich indicated he was told by his handler that the Soviets would only trust him if they believed his cover story that he needed the money to cover some debts. Those debts as set forth in court proceedings were $500 and $700.

It is unrefuted that the U.S. Army vetted him before providing him with the top-secret clearance that he had. He was groomed for the position and well-trained. Yet with this background and a near genius IQ, *The Times* article implied that Helmich was not smart enough to cover a few small overdrafts and his only recourse was to commit espionage? That is the story the U.S. Government peddled.

The facts and evidence do not support that storyline.

Helmich scoffed at the suggestion that he had to commit an act of espionage to cover a few overdrafts. He indicated to me and detailed in his manuscript that he was thoroughly recruited and taught spycraft by his handlers who identified themselves and produced documentation that they were officers of the CIA.

He recounted being presented with a letter addressed to him from Richard Helms, then Deputy Director of the CIA, as to the importance of his mission.

Helmich second-guessed himself during our conversation. He questioned if perhaps the letter itself may have been false and this was all part of an effort by Soviet moles to set him up to believe he served the CIA. Helmich struggled with the possibility that he was set up.

But despite the self-reflection, Helmich firmly believed that he assisted the CIA to perform these services and spent months training for the assignment as well as creating his cover story to convince the Soviets of his motivation. He indicated that he was excited to get the opportunity to assist the CIA in this action. He voluntarily released this information to the FBI over months of debriefing and felt that his undisclosed role as a CIA operative would be recognized for what it was. It was not.

Helmich lamented to me (and indicated as much in his manuscript) that if he was wrong on this then he was in fact duped by the Soviet military intelligence who ran their own cover story on him to recruit him and to secure his services. What Helmich explained to me debunked the disinformation stories I read and the narrative the Prosecution advanced of this poorly educated lone-wolf traitor.

My takeaway from my discussions with Helmich (and my review of his manuscript) was that he was recruited for this assignment rather than the disinformation that this all evolved by happenstance since he wrote a few bad checks.

It was logical for me to conclude that some organization knew well in advance that it was essential for the Soviets to be able to see top-secret U.S. messages directly after Kennedy was assassinated. No coincidence here. This all was masterfully planned by some organization. And surely not some one-off act by a person who simply had to cover a few bad checks.

Sitting across the table from Helmich and discussing what he did, how he did it and why was eye opening.

For example, why did the Prosecution not even discuss the timing of the espionage act for which Helmich was charged? That this scenario had been orchestrated so the Soviets would have all the components of the KL-7 System and then were provided with the key codes and would have this information directly after the assassination. The key codes were changed periodically. So, for that brief window of time after the assassination, the Soviets, having active crypto codes, had a real-time look behind the curtain of U.S. Military intelligence.

After discussing this with Helmich and applying logic and inductive and deductive reasoning from the evidence I reviewed, including his manuscript, it led me to these inescapable conclusions:

A. Helmich was a highly intelligent operative, well trained in spycraft and his manuscript identified in detail the times, places and events for these covert operations. There was no army record of him having training in counterintelligence, yet the U.S. Government admitted in the court proceedings that he was assigned to the ASA in Viet Nam which had a counterintelligence unit.

B. He surely was no lone-wolf actor.

C. The series of espionage acts were not caused by Helmich passing a few bad checks.

D. This series of events was well-orchestrated by multiple parties.

E. The events leading up to Helmich's actions on Nov. 22, 1963 were planned well in advance.

F. The surrender of top-secret key codes enabled the Soviets to monitor U.S. Military communications during that turbulent and critical period following the assassination.

G. The ability of the Soviets to monitor U.S. top-secret information directly after the assassination prevented any misunderstanding that there would be an escalation of tensions during the Cold War or a retaliation strike that could have started World War III, which almost happened just the year before during the Cuban Missile Crisis.

H. The Soviets had the key codes and were able to confirm that there would be no reprisals for the assassination, and no repeat of the Cuban Missile Crisis.

I. This was a well-thought-out plan, carried out and timed perfectly.

J. Someone or some organization planned all of this well in advance to place a wall around the assassination.

K. Helmich, like so many others involved, could be blamed as a lone-wolf actor.

This was no wild conspiracy theory of espionage that I heard. The facts and events surrounding Helmich's espionage activities were the centerpiece of the Prosecution's case in which they obtained a verdict. Yet the significance of the event and the timing of the act was never discussed once Helmich pled guilty.

These facts were never exposed. All of the information was there. Hidden in plain sight. Helmich, by his plea agreement, was doomed to a life sentence, which was the worst-case scenario had he presented his defense and lost.

CHAPTER 13

Finding Jean Helmich

REVISITING THE PAST
ELICITS PAINFUL MEMORIES

It took time to find Jean Helmich.

In 2019, I finally located Joseph Helmich's widow in of all places, the sleepy little town of Keystone Heights, Fla., population 1,478. Keystone Heights is located in central Florida's Clay County.

I was pretty excited to find Jean after all these years. I thought she would be excited when I told her of Joe's manuscript and the declassification of his FBI file. I assumed she would be as interested as I was to finally share this information. Such would not be the case.

Cordial when I called, Jean was adamant that she did not want anything to do with Joe's manuscript or reliving the story. She never read it nor even heard of it. She did not want to open this case up based upon the tremendous heartache and horrible memories she experienced and endured all these years.

She clearly did not want to bring more attention to herself. Like someone who has been terribly abused, Jean did not want to mentally return to that place. Those memories were too painful to revisit.

As I listened to Jean, I realized how oblivious I had been to the pain this entire matter inflicted on her and her son. I realized I was insensitive to what she went through. I had not considered how much this had affected Jean.

I was interested in finally releasing this information. Jean was interested in surviving.

Jean literally suffered the life of Job after Joe's conviction. She was ostracized by society. Her own family turned her away. Labeled as being married to a Soviet spy.

There were beliefs she was also complicit because she accompanied her husband on the flight from the United States to Paris on Nov. 22, 1963 where her husband turned over top secrets to the Soviets. She vividly recalled that flight. She initially was so happy to be taking a trip to Paris with her husband. That happiness would later turn to sadness.

She flew with Joe Helmich that fateful day and heard the pilot's announcement that Kennedy was killed. She cried like all Americans did and mourned the loss of our President.

But to her family and friends she was as much complicit as Joe or the individuals who scheduled him to be on that flight.

Everyone assumed she profited from the money her husband received and for which he served a life sentence. That tax-free payment was equivalent to $1.3 million in 2025 dollars. The government also charged that Helmich received payments equivalent to $300,000 in 2025 dollars (again tax free) for espionage acts in Mexico and Viet Nam.

Jean denied any involvement, but she has been forever branded with Joe's conviction as if it was tattooed across her forehead: Wife of a traitor and Soviet spy!

As she explained her situation, I thought why would she want to participate in advancing the release of the manuscript? Her tragic memories of this event destroyed the only happiness that she ever had and ruined the rest of her life.

Jean has no trust in government agencies and the national media, which excoriated her husband and her life. Jean recounted all this in an in-depth interview we did with her to get her thoughts recorded. We hoped she would reconsider and change her mind on releasing Helmich's manuscript. I would not release the information without her blessing. At that time, it did not seem she would ever provide that consent.

I was patient. I slowly advised Jean of the importance of the manuscript and the information it could provide to others who spent years of their lives putting together clues on the assassination of the 35th President of the United States.

I explained that some of the information in Joe's manuscript could be useful to those dedicated to uncovering information on the Kennedy Assassination. The information Helmich revealed in his *KAK: Manuscript*, when combined with other evidence, could in fact lead to more information being revealed or disclosed. Perhaps someone else would come forward and that person might have information of their own to share and would do so once the *KAK: Manuscript* was released.

The information that the manuscript could provide might be lynchpin evidence when added to the massive amount of what already has been discovered and is being discovered as the Kennedy Assassination files are being released.

The release of the *KAK: Manuscript* would provide some additional evidence and shed light on the fact that a group of individuals knew in advance that Kennedy was going to be assassinated. That is one piece of critical information as to the assassination.

The perpetrators had no concern of how evil their deed was in and of itself. Their concern was to ensure that this assassination did not create worldwide panic, repercussions with the Soviets or World War III. Their concern was to have a change of the guard with minimal loss of life, other than Kennedy's. Any witnesses who had knowledge of the assassination also were expendable.

It took quite some time, but Jean finally relented and decided to get behind the release of Joe Helmich's story and his manuscript in hopes of setting the record straight, telling her late husband's story, as well as, providing the public with another piece of the Kennedy Assassination puzzle. With her blessing, we started our research project and the writing of this book.

The *KAK: Manuscript* and the backstory from my interview with

Helmich reveals an interesting behind-the-scenes look at the actions taken by Joseph G. Helmich during a tumultuous time in our country's history, which many people feel was a significant negative turning point for the United States.

Helmich's activities on Nov. 22, 1963 and his manuscript certainly are missing pieces supporting the conspiracy theory that someone or some organization knew well in advance that there would be an assassination of President Kennedy and used Helmich as part of an operation to defuse any issues with our then Cold War enemy, the Soviet Union.

The information also could defuse the construct that the most powerful man in the world was assassinated by a lone-wolf gunman with no involvement of any other organizations or country. That all of this was just the result of some cosmic coincidence of all of these details falling into place to allow Lee Harvey Oswald to be the lone shooter to take Kennedy off the board. Silencing the witnesses to the conspiracy by murder or threat of murder is an essential part of the coup as we saw happen with Oswald. The release of this information may provide meaning to their deaths.

CHAPTER 14

Jean Helmich

ABANDONMENT BY FAMILY AND SOCIETY LEAD TO A SORROWFUL LIFE

Jean Helmich believed in her husband Joe because he loved her unconditionally. It is something she said she never experienced before.

It is one of the few fond memories she holds on to, now living alone in her late 80s.

As a youth, Jean felt unloved and unwanted. Her parents did not get along. As a result, there is a portion of her young life she said she blocked out.

When Jean's mother got pregnant and told her father, he did not believe the child was his.

"Unfortunately, I was a spitting image of his mom," she said. "He could not get out of that but he never really did anything."

Jean's mother was tired of traveling west with him. She said, "We leave again, I'm going to divorce you."

One night, Jean's father went to work as a night watchman and did not return home. "We figured he got on the railroad and left us," she said.

He did ultimately return to see family. Jean felt her father not only did not want her but he did not want his wife to have her. In addition, Jean's mom seemed to blame Jean for her marital problems.

As a result, she vividly remembers the sorrow of being placed in a foster home at age 7, abandoned by her mother and father. "I didn't grow up with my mother," she said. "My dad deserted us. I never felt love from anybody until Joe."

Jean stayed in foster care for more than 10 years, having to reconcile that both her parents had so little love for her that they would give her away to a state-run foster home. This is trauma with a deep wound.

Jean said she's a survivor and not a victim. There's a saying, "what doesn't kill you makes you stronger." She is the epitome of the American spirit, never giving up even though her adversary - the U.S. Government - was in a far superior position to suppress her knowledge of what took place with her husband.

Jean left foster care and started a life of her own. Joseph Helmich met her while she taught dance at the Fred Astaire Studio in Augusta, Ga.

"We're not supposed to date our students but we were hardly having business," she said. "I accepted and he asked me where I lived. He didn't tell me what he was doing."

Jean chuckled at that memory.

She did know her husband received top-secret clearance from the U.S. Army. Instead of asking Jean to marry him, Joe said, "I have orders to go to France – and I want you to come with me."

"And as far as he was concerned, that settled everything," Jean said.

The two married in 1957. They soon moved to Paris, where they lived from 1958 to 1963.

Jean didn't like France for a variety of reasons. They lived in a block house the Germans had built in World War II. She also found the French to be extremely rude.

"Every time I tried to learn, they laughed so I said, 'To hell with you,'" she said. If she'd learn a language, it would be German. "My family's great grandparents were German," she said. "And Joe's family was from there."

Jean and Joe had returned to the United States for just a few months. They were stationed in Fort Bragg, N.C. in the Fall of 1963 when his CIA contact told him to fly to Paris between Nov. 20 and Nov. 25, as Joe indicated in his manuscript.

"Likely it will be on Nov. 22," the CIA handler told Joe.

Two days before he left, Helmich wrote that his CIA contact confirmed "the 22nd was the date of travel and, if at all possible, to be on the way to Paris Orly Airport by 9 a.m."

Jean said she accompanied her husband on Nov. 22, 1963. When they flew over rural Virginia, the pilot told passengers that President Kennedy had been assassinated. She recalled the extreme sadness she felt and noted a number of people on the plane were crying.

"When we landed, Joe made a phone call to see if they wanted him to come back," Jean recalled. "And they said, 'No, go ahead,' which I thought was kind of weird." During the call, Helmich wrote in his manuscript that his handler advised him that it was extremely important that Helmich conclude his mission and deliver the current top-secret key codes to the Soviets.

Jean said she was not aware of what he was doing. After they landed and reached their hotel late on November 22, Joe advised her that he had to meet some people the following morning.

The morning following Kennedy's assassination, Helmich delivered the remaining components of the KL-7 cryptograph machine and the then current key code list to the Soviets. Joe Helmich - in his position as a cryptographer receiving, reviewing and forwarding all of the top-secret communications - knew how close we were to World War III at the time. He divulged that fact in his manuscript while handling the frantic military intelligence communications during the Cuban Missile Crisis. Helmich read in real time and had first-hand knowledge of how the U.S. inched closer to a possible nuclear war.

Soviet deployments of nuclear missiles in Cuba matched American deployments of nuclear missiles in Italy and Turkey. President Kennedy staved off a nuclear confrontation, but as Joe Helmich wrote, the deal he made to block the invasion of Cuba to avoid WWWIII infuriated top military officials. That was another factor in the demise of President Kennedy.

Jean said the FBI gave her its story on what took place in Paris in 1963 and Joe gave her his.

She said she doesn't know exactly what was accurate but she believed in her husband. She had no knowledge nor was she involved in the transfer of military secrets.

The U.S. Government never charged Jean with conspiracy or any involvement in the espionage acts of her husband. When Jean told me that Joe excitedly first informed her that the CIA recruited him in Paris, she said she warned him in no uncertain terms, "Don't get involved with the CIA."

That warning went unheeded.

In 1964, Jean was supposed to accompany Joe to Mexico City but she didn't want to go. Replacing her was Joe's stepfather, Rick Helmich, a retired U.S. Army veteran. Joe Helmich said that he met his CIA contact and observed the assassination of an undercover operative working in Mexico City.

Blackmail With Consequences

After the FBI arrested Joe, his pre-trial hearing started on Aug. 25, 1981. Jean followed the case intently and communicated with her jailed husband during the trial.

While in jail and awaiting trial, Joe told his wife that he would not admit to being a spy and indicated he would present his entire case once the prosecutors presented theirs. Jean shared what Joe had told her, which was consistent with what Joe wrote in his manuscript.

But on Sept. 28, the day after the Prosecution rested its case and just before the Defense presented its position, Joe abruptly and surprisingly confessed to one of the four counts. He pleaded guilty to conspiring with the Soviet Union to sell them top-secret U.S. Military intelligence and decoding equipment.

"Then all of a sudden, the next day in court, he pled guilty," Jean said. "I didn't know what happened. We got to see him downstairs, we were right with him. I said, 'What's going on?'

"So, he told me, 'Well, I got a phone call last night after the government rested their case.' They told him what they'd do to us if it continued. So, he decided to plead guilty. He felt he had no choice since our lives were threatened."

The Helmich files contained an affidavit of Jean Helmich (BILLIE JEAN nee Johnson HELMICH) that stated under oath she discovered a sealed letter from Joe Helmich written in September 1980 - a year before he was arrested - that indicated his life was threatened by "some U.S. Government agent or official" ... "And that he clearly expected to be killed if he did not cooperate with the FBI."

The affidavit was sent to Federal Court Judge Susan Black and further went on to state under oath by Jean Helmich that "At this meeting my husband told Mr. Dcaring (Hclmich's court appointcd defense counsel) and I that he had been informed that he could not leave the trial "alive and free."

Helmich wrote in his manuscript that he specifically advised his wife of this situation. He told me the same thing in my interview with him at FCI Talladega.

Specifically, he said that he was told by his CIA handler that if he revealed any of the information as part of his defense - which arguably could have raised the reasonable doubt standard and avoided a verdict of guilty - that he would immediately learn that his wife and son were killed. After that they indicated his own death would promptly follow.

By Helmich pleading guilty, the Justice Department dropped all of the charges but one. However, he still had to serve a life sentence since the U.S. Government did not live up to its promise to suggest parole after 10 years due to his cooperation. Why give up your right to defend when there was no death penalty? Why plead to one life sentence when the worst that could happen is multiple life sentences. Helmich was never going to get paroled. Not for those claimed acts. The U.S. Government would never let him leave prison alive, one life sentence, two, three or four.

Jean said that in addition to the threats, Joe told her that government people promised that she and her son would have financial assistance if he pled guilty.

"Joe told me they told him if he pleaded guilty, we would have so much money," Jean said. "They also said, 'He shouldn't be in any more than 15 years.'"

That again, as Jean said, was a "pack of lies." The shortened sentence that Helmich believed he would receive didn't happen. He would serve every remaining day he was alive in prison.

Joe Helmich died in the Bureau of Prisons facility on Nov. 26, 2002. Two days before Thanksgiving, more than 21 years after his plea and more than 39 years after Kennedy's assassination.

"We didn't receive money," Jean said. "No help. When I left Jacksonville, Fla., going to Augusta, Ga. to see my mother, I was followed. I was followed home. I'm not stupid, not as stupid as they thought I was.

"So, I would like to know why the government likes to lie so much. I've gotten to the point; I don't trust them anymore. I don't trust my own government."

Jean also grew to resent newspaper reporters and the media spin on the events. They overlooked facts that were in plain sight, such as the timing of the turnover of the secret information to the Soviets the day after the Kennedy Assassination and the significant amount paid to get this information.

"I said, 'You're all a bunch of vultures,'" she said. "They dug into every piece of dirt they could go by. As far as I was concerned, when I said, 'A bunch of vultures,' I meant it. I also said, 'You're damn lucky they didn't do this to you.'"

The national publicity of the trial painted Joe Helmich as a traitor and a person to be despised. That national publicity also shone onto Jean and negatively affected her life.

On top of the tragedy of her husband's conviction, Jean said Joe's family "turned on her." Rick Helmich told the FBI's Harry Robinson that, "She and her son will have a home with us," only to renege on the offer two days later, according to Jean.

"Joe's mother came home and said, 'Rick wants to know when you're going to be leaving,' Jean recalled. "She said, 'It's too hard on him having you in the home.' "

So, Jean was yet again abandoned by family members, this time Joe's family in a time of need and desperation.

Jean didn't fare much better with her own family who likewise shunned her. Everywhere she went, once people realized who she was they immediately reacted and created problems for her. Jean never changed her last name, proudly defying those who attacked her to keep the name of her first and only love.

Jean's life has been dramatically affected.

She has lived like a pauper while regularly having to move. She lives on Social Security and whatever assistance she can get. She lives alone and still takes care of herself. She is strong and proud but has been beaten down her entire life. Her once bright time of her life was her marriage with Joe.

Jean literally has lived the life of Job. The only joy she had was her time with Joe during their marriage, which ended when Joe was arrested.

As for her husband, she was asked in an interview if she still believes in him.

"Yeah, I'll continue to stand by him, God willing," she said.

TURBULENT TIMES

CHAPTER 15

America In The
Fall Of 1963

SUPREME CONFIDENCE ON THE PRECIPICE OF
A MAJOR WAR THAT FOREVER CHANGES SOCIETY

The 1960s: A time of absolute national confidence. America had won World War II. We were the only true dominant country in the world with the most sophisticated military and the strongest economy of any nation on Earth.

We were the envy of the world. And my generation grew up in that world. Young men filled with hope and vigor. We felt fully able to take on all comers at any costs. We grew up in America while all these events swirled around us.

My generation idolized John F. Kennedy. So did the American public. The Deep State had to contend with Kennedy's popularity because pundits felt he had a great chance of winning a second term.

The three Presidents before him - Franklin Roosevelt, Harry Truman and Dwight Eisenhower - all served at least two terms. Even though he had a razor-thin victory at the polls when first elected, over the whole of his presidency, Kennedy averaged a 70 percent approval rating, comfortably the highest of any post-World War II president. By comparison, the average for all Presidents between 1938 and 2012 was 54 percent.

So objectively, it was no stretch to believe he would win a second term. Recall that Kennedy's popular brother Bobby was his attorney general and pundits felt RFK could succeed JFK.

Then there was also Ted Kennedy, who managed his brother's campaign in the western states before becoming a U.S. Senator in 1962. The Kennedy dominance could have been expected to continue for years.

That was also a reality the Deep State considered.

Keep that in context as events rapidly unfolded leading up to the Kennedy Assassination.

At the beginning of the Kennedy administration, the U.S. Military had serious issues with him during his first term when he did not give full support to the Bay of Pigs Invasion. The CIA in particular was livid that Kennedy did not want this mission to even go off.

Started without Kennedy's support, the mission failed. Those promoting the Bay of Pigs Invasion, proceeded without authorization from the President. Per historians, Kennedy felt he was misled, although he personally accepted the blame in the famous address to the nation in which he stated, "Victory has a thousand fathers, but Defeat is an orphan."

Robert F. Kennedy Jr., in an interview with podcaster Joe Rogan in 2024, recalled his uncle John F. Kennedy telling family members how furious he was with the CIA. He said the following after leaving a meeting where he determined that he had been misled about the invasion: "I want to smash the CIA into a million pieces and scatter it into the winds."

The President sets foreign policy as is his constitutional role. There was a major division happening between what Kennedy wanted and the direction the Deep State wanted. The CIA boldly pushed the invasion of Cuba without Presidential support and assumed Kennedy would be forced to order air support, knowing that without it, the invasion would fail.

Kennedy refused to accept the position that the CIA forced him into, did not escalate the invasion and gave no air support. The invasion forces were trapped on the Cuban beaches where they were killed or captured. This was a disastrous failure. The repercussions would be severe.

There was no denying Kennedy's displeasure with the CIA overstepping its role and invading another country with no Presidential or Congressional authorization.

After the event historians identified a group in the military and in the CIA that felt Kennedy was taking us down the wrong path. They wrote that the military and U.S. intelligence agencies believed they had their own duty to protect the country, possibly even from Kennedy himself.

Their approach directly opposed Kennedy's vision. It is logical to consider that these actors decided that at some point Kennedy would need to be removed in the same manner the CIA previously had used. The CIA had been instrumental in regime change by removing numerous other political leaders throughout the world in the 20th century.

These events formed a logical foundation that a select number of our military leaders and representatives of our intelligence agencies opposed Kennedy. They also planned a regime change in the United States.

There was major mistrust and, in some instances, documented efforts to undermine Kennedy's policies. Throughout history, starting from Roman times, political conspiracies existed. A political conspiracy refers to a group of people united in the goal of overthrowing an established political leader.

That defines what I believe happened in America in 1963.

Those factors may rationally explain why the Kennedy Assassination on Nov. 22, 1963 happened. Some historians opined that the military and intelligence circles felt Kennedy did not represent the United States' best interest around the world with his calls for peace and disarmament. In the face of a massive communist push worldwide for domination, many in the Deep State felt Kennedy compromised our national security.

Consider that the Deep State may have felt Kennedy was too young, too inexperienced or too weak. Or perhaps any combination of those traits which disqualified him in their eyes to meet the security demands facing the United States. Maybe they rationalized, as they did with other deposed leaders, that his policies did not serve the national interest, so they determined Kennedy had to be removed.

In 1960, America changed swiftly when Kennedy was elected. From eight years of Republican leadership, with Eisenhower being the former commander of the entire military, to a much younger successor with his own progressive worldview. A view that was distinctly different than the standard that existed before he took office.

Did the Deep State have enough resentment to mount an assassination attempt? That premise must be considered. That suggestion is more logical than the blind acceptance of the Warren Commission's findings.

When one looks back objectively on what took place at the time, it is no stretch to consider that the military and many other influential leaders may have felt that Kennedy established a position, which posed a clear and present danger to the United States. To use the current parlance, Kennedy may have been viewed as an "existential threat" by the Deep State. Its opinion of Kennedy as an "existential threat" could have formed the basis that no options were off the table, including assassination.

The Deep State had its position, and Kennedy was adamant about his view. Supported by his handpicked, brilliant staff of top thinkers in America, dubbed the "best and brightest," Kennedy believed his approach was the correct path for America.

Kennedy and his advisors advanced "brilliant policies that defied common sense" as noted by one author. Specifically, those policies on Viet Nam as advocated by Kennedy's assemblage of academics and intellectuals diverged from the policies of the then-existing U.S. Department of State officials and military advisors, as it related to Viet Nam.

Clearly there was a basis for the Deep State to feel that the actions of Kennedy, as advocated by his advisors, was not the correct direction for our country from their perspective. Kennedy was not shy about advancing his dream of world peace and did so in a brilliant manner. He did not want to engage in protracted, endless wars. That set the stage for a confrontation.

John F. Kennedy spoke eloquently and inspired the country and the youth of America. His speechwriters prepared flawless and moving speeches, which Kennedy delivered with supreme confidence and clarity. Any person who listened to those speeches had to be moved in some way, regardless of political bent.

Kennedy asked all of us to contribute to the growth and success of our country. His speeches were aspirational as well as inspirational. Kennedy made us all believers. He made us believe his dream of world peace could possibly happen.

In his Presidential inauguration speech on January 20, 1961, he boldly challenged all citizens, imploring people to, "Ask not what your country can do for you - ask what you can do for your country." He requested the youth to consider service to the country and the world. Kennedy challenged us to accept responsibility to protect the principles upon which America was founded.

Less than six weeks after his inauguration, President Kennedy issued an executive order establishing the Peace Corps as a pilot program within the Department of State. His themes of self-sacrifice and volunteerism were a driving force behind the creation of the Peace Corps. The Peace Corps' purpose was to promote world peace and friendship by helping countries in need of trained manpower, particularly in the poorest areas.

Kennedy encouraged and in fact challenged the youth of America to accept responsibility for protecting the principles that our country was founded upon. A positive message to my generation, not for self-gain but to act in the best interest of our country and the world.

My generation believed nothing could go wrong with our young commander at the helm. Kennedy reinforced that positive message with his own words, actions and expressed intentions toward world disarmament. He painted an optimistic and strong view of America prospering and growing. It was not the view shared by many in charge of the military industrial complex who felt the winds of war and were anticipating the next military conflict. Kennedy's vision on foreign policy was not viewed by some as the appropriate stance for our country.

The U.S. had been embroiled in the Korean War. The Cold War was underway. Kennedy did not plan on starting another endless war on his watch and clearly didn't want to escalate military activities in Viet Nam.

That was an agenda the old guard wanted to advance.

The speeches by Kennedy support what most historians and political observers agree upon: a full-blown war effort in Viet Nam was never Kennedy's goal. Kennedy's ultimate goal was in fact not war but withdrawal from Viet Nam as evidenced by National Security Action Memo 26 approved by Kennedy six weeks before he was killed.

Kennedy also advanced his agenda for world disarmament which reflected Kennedy's views on war. I am certain that his "Pax Americana" speech at America University in the Spring of 1963 evoked a visceral response by the war hawks in the government. Kennedy recognized the problems in South Viet Nam, he had his own concepts of how to address those issues and was not advocating in any way a full-blown military invasion of Viet Nam to support the South Viet Nam regime.

With the assistance of his advisors, Kennedy became forward thinking on future military engagements around the world and in Viet Nam, such as the use of U.S. Special Forces to lead operations with strategic goals in mind. He wanted to use air power and special operations forces, such as the Green Berets, to fight guerrilla wars.

A client who I interviewed while preparing this book served in Viet Nam. He was a U.S. Army Officer and Green Beret. He related that CIA operatives in Viet Nam and military leadership were not receptive to Kennedy's concepts of using Special Forces over traditional forces to fight these guerilla wars.

A reason for the pushback? This would block the broad war effort, which some in the military establishment wanted. From the view of the Deep State, military spending would be far less for surgical air strikes and focused operations vs. a major war. Less expenditures result in less profits for the military industrial complex, simple as that.

While some applauded the concept of using Special Forces to fight guerilla wars, some of the top brass in the military did not accept these new concepts of counter-insurgency warfare coming from only a former junior officer in the Navy like Kennedy.

The irony is thick because the concept of using Special Forces with surgical land and air strikes has now been adopted as a standard warfare strategy by many in the military. We now embrace the missions of Seal Teams and other Special Forces.

However, the Deep State saw an enemy on the march in world communism and felt what needed to be done was a more expansive response instead of adopting the concept of Special Forces in a timely fashion.

They wanted their next big war. Kennedy would not give it to them.

Keep in mind, our societal structure differed back then. Our country in the 1960s was vastly more conservative compared to the contrast of the Republican and Democratic parties in 2025. The Democratic party back then was far more moderate and centrist on the political spectrum. Kennedy also advocated a strong stance for civil rights, which created a societal shift needed. However, with all such change comes resistance.

I want the younger generations reading this book to be aware of our country's history at the time. In the case of the Kennedy Assassination, they need to understand the events taking place at the time that affected our country, along with the actions and reactions that the U.S. Government took to respond to those events.

I want these generations to consider the possibility that a group of individuals or organizations operating in this country could justify such an evil deed as the assassination of our President under the guise of national security. I also want them to recognize that the ends will never justify the means regardless of the rationalization of national security.

As I have identified with objective facts and without emotion, the concept of Kennedy's assassination being carried out with the knowledge and approval of a group of individuals and organizations is far more logical, albeit harder to accept as an American, than accepting the Warren Commission's lone gunman theory.

We need to recognize the historical setting the country was in to enable the generations that come after us to understand one explanation of how power could be wielded, even to the extent of the President of the United States being assassinated under the guise of being done for the greater good. Consider that even in 2025, the power of the Deep State controls many of the decisions being made in our country. The generations growing up in America in 2025 need to keep an open mind to events occurring around us and question who is controlling the direction of the country.

From a personal perspective, I wanted to provide a glimpse of what my thoughts were - and the thoughts that many from my generation shared - during this troubled time. While world and national events were intense, the youth in America were brimming with confidence and had a positive attitude about ourselves.

The youth of America were ready to step up to not only take our place in America, but in the world. My generation of Americans embodied the indomitable spirit of being an American and young citizen in the greatest country on Earth.

CHAPTER 16

Under A Cloud Of War

THE YOUNG WARRIOR CLASS IN AMERICA
GROWING UP IN THE 1960s

My generation of young men faced an exciting time as we grew up in America.

We identified with the youthful John F. Kennedy, who led our country and inspired us to believe that the future was wide open. I recall my older brother and his friends in the mid-1960s before the full ramp up of the Viet Nam War, displaying supreme confidence. In fact, dominance was the attitude of my generation, and this prideful energy prevailed throughout our country.

Simply put, our generation believed we were the best.

No limits.

We were the generation living at the best time in the greatest country in the history of the world.

Kennedy challenged our country that we would be on the Moon by the end of the decade. Nothing was out of reach.

At the same time, those born in this era recall that we were the first generation that lived under the threat of nuclear annihilation and we were given repeated warnings in school such as 'duck and cover' under our school desks in the event of a nuclear attack. We were unfazed by those warnings.

Cars And Girls

Bringing the times into perspective, what got all young men excited - other than chasing girls - was Muscle Cars. My brother's friends all had a passion for working on their cars: Pontiac GTOs, the SS 396 Camaro, Chevy Impala 409 and the Dodge Ramcharger just to name a few.

My favorite, which actually did not fit the muscle car label since it was in a category of its own, was the Corvette Stingray. The styling of the Stingray at the time seemed something out of a science fiction movie. Just looking at its profile set it apart from other cars on the road.

I recall my brother Ken getting a midnight blue 1963 split-window Corvette Stingray shortly before he deployed to Viet Nam. The Stingray name was first used on the Corvette built in 1963. The ultimate car for America. No one in the world had what we had. This car was far ahead of its time in style and no other car came close to the Stingray for looks. I had the opportunity to drive that car when I was 16. The thrill can't be described.

On his return from Viet Nam, my brother bought what at the time was absolutely the car on the top of the muscle car food chain: The Chevy Camaro 427 or more specifically the Chevy Camaro L72 427. That car was rated as having 425 horsepower, but many experts believe it was far more powerful than that.

My brother Ken bought this garnet red rocket from the Ed Stinn Chevy dealership in Cleveland, which originally bought it to put it on the track for competitive drag racing. There were only 1,000 Camaros in the country that left the factory outfitted like the one my brother bought.

I was also lucky enough to be able to drive that car. In my first and only drive, I floored it to hit full throttle. It was hard to keep that car from fishtailing due to the tremendous power transferred to the rear tires. It seemed like it burned rubber forever.

What a rush!

Later in that ride with my brother sitting shotgun, we ended up at a stoplight next to a Corvette - of all cars to match up with. The driver looked over at us and may have thought this was a normal Camaro. The other driver and I both revved our engines, so it was game on for a drag race. We blew the doors off that Corvette. The American Muscle Car! Accept no substitutes.

Full disclosure on muscle cars: As much as I admired muscle cars, I never was able to afford one or own one. My dad bought my first car as a surprise the summer before my senior year in high school when I was 16.

At the time, our family finances were on a downward trend as a result of my father, a supermarket owner, challenging the unionization of his store by the Retail Clerks Union. My dad was an extremely fair employer. When confronted with the demand by the union, he had all of the employees take a vote. To a person they voted against the union.

However, daily picketing in a heavy union town with housewives confronted as they pulled in to shop resulted in a dramatic drop off in customers.

My dad was unmercifully harassed by the union organizers. I recall the constant calls to our home late at night and my father's face as he had to hear the union threats. That was one battle my brave dad did not win and forced him to sell his business.

It eventually required my parents to also sell the beautiful home I grew up in to move into an apartment. In some ways, our family's plight resembled Joseph Helmich's. We faced powerful forces that we couldn't overcome.

Given that context of family finances, I would get no new muscle car or, in fact, no new car at all in my future.

My dad, along with his friend and insurance agent Jimmy Janasko, located a vehicle at an estate sale and bought it as my first car. My dad surprised me by parking the car in my grandparents' garage for the big reveal. My grandparents never owned a car but did have a garage.

With excitement, I opened the door to the garage to see a 9-year-old used 1957 Imperial two-door coupe built by Chrysler, which was bought from a recently deceased elderly lady's estate. Most disheartening, the car was light pink or "shell pink" with a white top. Clearly a nice elderly lady's ride, but no muscle car. Certainly not a car any boy my age would want to drive as his first car. At the time my only transportation was a Schwinn three-speed bike so regardless, this was a big step up in transportation for me.

My dad saw the disappointed look on my face and told me it was either the car or I could continue pedaling my bike. Great proposal. I immediately took the keys from his hand and muttered a half-hearted thank you. I realized some years later how ungrateful I must have appeared. I never considered that this was the best gift my dad could afford at the time.

With that Imperial, I was 16 years old going on 90. That was my 'A Boy Named Sue' car since I sure caught a lot of static from my teammates when I pulled up at summer football practice in that pink-and-white ride. I eventually laughed all of that off and discovered that it was the ultimate dating car. The extra wide full seats front and back had a significant advantage on a date.

Thanks Dad.

Independence Day

I decided to make some more lemonade with that car. I put a trailer hitch on the rear. Reese Morgan, a good friend and teammate on my high school football team, decided he and I would take the Imperial camping. Reese became an outstanding high school football coach in Iowa, then later an outstanding position coach at the University of Iowa. He was also a badass.

I knew that Reese and I would be a formidable pair if we got into any trouble on the trip and we had no fear about a week in the wilderness. However, just to make sure, I packed my 20-gauge shotgun and my .22 semi-automatic pistol.

We hooked a camper to the rear of that Imperial. I made that car into my personal pink-and-white F-150.

We weren't just going on a local camping trip. We were going international. We drove the Imperial to Algonquin Provincial Park in Ontario, Canada, which is literally a 3,000-square-mile forest of hills and lakes. I failed to recognize that transporting firearms across the Canadian border exposed us to a fine and potential first offender status of jail time for up to two years.

We spent a week camping out, hiking, working out, canoeing, and just exploring what to us was a new wilderness. We were doing what most young American men my age did.

The information on the campsite inside Algonquin Park where we stayed was that it was rare to encounter bears. We encountered bears our first night. A bear woke us up when it ransacked our campsite and tent due to us not taking adequate precautions with our food supply.

Lesson learned. What a rush!

We had a great time. All went well until we were leaving. We felt wc just conquered the wilderness in another country. As I drove, I kept seeing these large 4x6 Canadian flags flying from 40-foot flagpoles at rest areas. I pulled the Imperial over and told Reese we were taking the Canadian flag to reflect our win over Canada. My idea, not his.

Immature, but a cocky 16-year-old, I climbed the 40-foot flagpole to cut down the Canadian flag as our victory trophy. Reese watched to see if I could make that climb. I did well, about three stories up when I looked down to see a truck with the unmistakable markings of the Canadian Mounted Police that we had previously seen. The officers were not happy with what they saw and interrogated both of us. I was sorry that I got Reese into that situation.

Neither Reese nor I admitted to anything, since in fact we had not committed any crime other than my transport of firearms across their border. We did not break during the interrogation. The Mounties searched the vehicle but did not search inside the mattress where I had stored our weapons.

The weapons were mine and to his credit, Reese did not give me up, even though during those separate interrogations, the Mounties promised us that if we told on the other person we could be released.

Typical tactic of investigative questioning. It did not work on either of us.

We were released and I do recall the last thing one of the Mounties told me: "Keep driving to the border and don't stop, even if it is for gas. If you run out of gas, then push your car across the border."

Looking back on that trip, my dad and mom allowing their teenage son to leave the country for a week to go camping in a Canadian forest was not out of the ordinary at the time for parents to approve, but probably not something most parents today would accept.

We, of course, had no cell phones. I don't recall ever calling home while we were gone. This was just what young men my age did in those times.

My generation took on challenges. Hiking in the hills and camping out a week in a huge forest in another country was probably good training for boot camp. Similar to what I did with my friends. We grew up playing war games in our neighborhood, shooting each other with our Daisy BB guns, much to the displeasure of our parents.

In high school we took it to another level, actually dividing up in teams and playing war games in the woods next to the Black River in East Lorain. The goal was to shoot your enemy with a BB gun or a pellet rifle, overcome their defenses and capture the other team's flag. Again, probably good training for those of us headed to the military.

I also took part in other outdoor activities like many young men. I worked construction in the summers while in high school for my uncle, Walt Jurczynski. Walt had three great sons, my cousins Bob, Rich and Walt Jr., who I considered additional older brothers. They taught me a lot and they all worked hard.

Walt's motto to my cousins growing up was, "If you don't work, you don't eat," which is a simple but motivating phrase.

I learned a lot from Uncle Walt and my cousins and will be forever grateful for that experience. Again, most of the friends I knew worked some type of job to earn additional money and working construction also had the added benefit of learning a trade and developing physically. Again, it gave us a purpose, we earned needed money and the hard work was good training for life. We were the young "warrior class" that all countries throughout history need to develop if they want to be a dominant force in the world.

North To Alaska

In the summer of 1969, at 18 years old, I was fortunate to land a construction job in the oil fields in Prudhoe Bay, Alaska, which is located on the shores of the Arctic Ocean. Prudhoe Bay is the largest oil field in the United States at over 200,000 acres and is located 250 miles north of the Arctic Circle on the northernmost part of Alaska. That job location at Prudhoc Bay (the "Slope" for those of us who worked there) was over 5,000 miles from my first job as an attorney on Fort Myers Beach, Fla., some years later.

The difference for those two jobs was stark: the frozen tundra of Prudhoe Bay vs. the white and warm sandy beaches of Southwest Florida. To put that into context, on my first day on the job in mid-August, it snowed as we started our day.

The Alaska job required our crew to work seven days a week, 12 hours a day. That's 84 hours of work, week after week. The normal rotations were six weeks on and then a week of rest and recuperation in Fairbanks.

Similar to what happens with servicemen deployed to a combat zone. Our crew lived in a construction trailer with no bathroom facilities about a mile from the main ARCO base camp at Prudhoe Bay where we ate and showered. It was a great experience for me as a young man growing up in America.

The work on the Slope was hard and at times dangerous. The Bureau of Labor Statistics indicates that fatalities in the normal workplace is three deaths per 100,000. But for workers in the oil and gas industry who work long hours around a lot of dangerous equipment, the death rate was more than five times higher than the normal job. We worked around dangerous equipment and conditions every day. You had to pay attention, especially if you were fatigued.

Toward the end of my tour on the Slope, I was in a building which was part of the oil platform. Our job was to apply protective coatings to the lines, pumps, tanks and other equipment inside the platform. We set up makeshift scaffolding to reach the upper areas of the building, about 30 feet in the air. We set down large 2x10 planks across the piping for our scaffold. Clearly not Occupational Safety and Health Administration (OSHA) compliant. And that makes sense as OSHA was not established until a year later.

We had general workplace safety rules in place but it was still dangerous. After placing the 2x10 plank you had to lay down black Visqueen on the plank to avoid overspray to the equipment some 30 feet below. I walked across the recently laid 2x10s carrying a large 2x10 and held it horizontally across my body with my arms wrapped over the plank as I walked it to extend our scaffold. I took a step onto what I thought was a plank covered in Visqueen when the bottom dropped out. There was no plank. I just stepped on a thin sheet of Visqueen with nothing below it other than a concrete floor and equipment.

I free fell a full body length when a miracle happened - the 2x10 slammed down on some piping below, jamming the plank into my armpits but stopping my fall.

I hung there dangling and holding onto the 2x10 until I was rescued. My foreman was pissed off. He asked me if I was injured, in which case I had to go to the base camp infirmary. We were 400 miles away from the nearest hospital. I told him that I was a little sore since my arms were badly bruised. My foreman then told me since I was not injured but just hurt that I should get back to work. I also received his safety advice as he told me, "And next time watch what the fuck you are doing!"

I got back to work and climbed back up to the elevated work area. Good life lesson: Sometimes in life you just have to work without a net.

There were also dangerous outdoor situations in Alaska to be cautious about. Since I was the rookie on the team, my job was to be first up at 4:30 a.m. and start the equipment and truck to warm them up for the day's work. In those early-morning hours in August in Alaska it was not truly dark but more like twilight.

On my first evening on the Slope at our construction trailer where we slept, I was handed a flashlight and told to grab a lug wrench. I understood what the flashlight was for but asked the foreman why I needed the lug wrench. He indicated that bears and wolves regularly roamed the area at night. Wolves and especially bears have a keen sense of smell and can detect urine from long distances. We had no toilets in our construction trailer so in the morning we would use the area outside to relieve ourselves. He knew I was a good athlete but he warned me not to run if attacked since I could never outrun the wolves or a bear if confronted. He also told me to carry the lug wrench so that if danger was approaching I would not be standing there with just my dick in my hand.

Great life lesson. I did learn to pay attention to my surroundings and be alert to fight if I had to. That was my morning ritual, every morning on the Slope.

I had some great moments while I was there.

I was able to see the Northern Lights one evening. Unbelievable colors and a once-in-a-lifetime experience.

I was at Prudhoe Bay during the attempted Northwest Passage effort by the tanker, the SS Manhattan. Opening a seaway for tankers to make their way from Alaska directly to Canadian and U.S. ports, was a historic event.

Our crew was asked to paint the symbolic golden oil drum reflecting the hope that this new Northwest Passage would open up passageways to deliver oil to Canada and the States. Our painted gold drum was the centerpiece of a ceremony for some oil executives and politicians when the SS Manhattan arrived. I played a small part in this historic event.

The concept of the "Northwest Passage" was an aspiration in 1969.

However if the Arctic's ice cap continues to recede at its current rate, the Northwest Passage may become a reality and expanding that concept to a "Northern Passage" may result in the shortest shipping route to Asia from North America.

That much sought-after "Northwest Passage" (now the "Northern Passage") may become a reality. President Trump has been in the forefront of these concepts and has laid the groundwork in early 2025 for acquisition of Greenland as part of an overall strategic policy for the United States. America is taking the lead on this historic new trade route.

Historically this is significant and President Trump's forward-thinking efforts reflect the wise Roman phrase, which in Latin is: "Audaces Fortuna Juvat": Fortune Favors the Bold.

I made awesome money working on the Slope, with pay for 40 hours, plus 44 hours overtime each week at time and a half. Due to my family finances and an error in judgment on my part, I needed the money to pay for next year's college expenses.

We left the Slope on Sept. 22, 1969 and I celebrated my 19th birthday having a number of hard-liquor drinks crossing the Arctic Circle on our way back to the States. Our roughneck crew did not need an excuse for having a drink. It was a great adventure and my crew gave me a framed certificate for crossing the Arctic Circle for my birthday.

All those experiences resembled what other young men in my generation did at that time.

We all spent a lot of time outdoors, engaged in sports or other activities and challenged ourselves every day. Some of us wanted to be rugged outdoorsmen or at least prove ourselves as men, so a transition from that life experience to a military boot camp or combat was different, but not foreign to what we had already learned as we grew up.

Similar to experiences I had, my brother and his friends hunted and fished. We all were taught to safely handle firearms and some of us became proficient marksmen, again, good training to enter the military.

Summer In America

And what would summer be without music? Endless summer songs by the Beach Boys. You could also hear the joyful Motown hits of The Temptations or Smokey Robinson, which we played on our car radios in Cleveland on CKLW (AM 800).

It would be a dozen years before George Strait had a country hit. Of course Jason Aldean, Kenny Chesney, Eric Church, Thomas Rhett and others weren't even born yet, so no country on the radio.

My brother and his friends, as stated, were supremely confident in their abilities, as most young men in America were back then. They were not shy about displaying their bravado, oftentimes engaging in fist fights to settle differences. That was the era I grew up in. It seemed like all of the guys in my generation had unlimited courage and looked forward to taking on challenges.

While I did admire my brother and his friends with how they could take apart and rebuild a car engine, I was into sports.

I tried to hang out with them from time to time. My brother was two years older than me, and some of his friends were either his age or a year or two older than him. Most of the teenagers his age in our town went to public high schools and the tough guys were members of clubs (law enforcement called them gangs). Their club names were the Bachelors, the Barons, the Dukes, the Cavaliers, etc. They all wore club jackets. Back in the day, I guess you could call them greasers.

High schoolers that I eventually went to school with were considered preppies or jocks. We wore letter sweaters, not gang jackets. We focused on getting ready for college and taking college prep courses. A good percentage of the public high school students were in vocational classes to get ready for their blue-collar jobs.

That is just the way it was. But greaser or preppie, our generation was cocky as to our place in the world. We were the up-and-coming generation in the No. 1 country in the world. We no doubt would dominate. All of us of course would answer the call, if necessary, to defend our country. Fighting was part of our nature in growing up. I wanted to take part.

There was one memorable night when I was allowed to join in: Fight Night. My brother had several of his friends in our basement taking turns boxing with eight-ounce gloves. I wanted to be part of the action.

My dad had taught me to box and I developed some skills. I defended myself well in the fights I got in. I was pretty confident and asked to put on the gloves to box with one of my brother's older friends. My request was granted. I started to box with an older and more developed young man than me. I did not know who he was. I would soon find out.

I was perhaps a little too confident taking this big step up in class with a bigger and older opponent.

Major mistake.

That is the first time I learned what it was like to be knocked out. As I was decked with what I was later told was a straight right to the jaw, my head bounced off the hard floor in our basement. I was knocked out for a few seconds, seeing the proverbial stars. My first concussion. The Rite of Passage for a young man at the time. I can recall that feeling even today.

My brother's friends quickly picked me up off the floor and told me I would be okay. They congratulated me on getting knocked out, which seemed odd at the time but I went with it. I was groggy and a bit wobbly with what I am sure was a shit-eating grin on my face. I laughed with them as they patted me on the back. I now joined them as a strong young man in America. They also told me I should be proud as to who I fought.

The young man I fought was about four years older than me and clearly more developed.

Unknown to me at the time, he was considered the toughest kid in South Lorain. That area was the roughest part of our city, close to our steel mill. He was "The Man."

My brother's friend who delivered the knockout shot to my jaw: Ray Hodorowski. In two years, he would become Lance Corporal Raymond Hodorowski, a machine gunner with the United States Marine Corps assigned to fight in Viet Nam.

Unfortunately, his other designation would soon be: Raymond Hodorowski, Killed In Action (KIA), Viet Nam, 1967.

This was the start of how I viewed Viet Nam.

That was my reality then.

Soon, it became the reality of many young men in America.

CHAPTER 17

The Viet Nam War

YOUNG AMERICANS WAIT THEIR TURN TO ENTER THE VALLEY OF THE SHADOW OF DEATH

In 1967, at the time of Ray Hodorowski's death, I was a junior in high school. I vividly remember attending Ray's funeral.

It was hard for me to comprehend how the toughest kid in my hometown could get killed. I thought he was indestructible. Ray was a badass. He was a lance corporal and machine gunner, killed in a mission called Operation Prairie II. Ray's last day alive was Monday, March 6, 1967. Ray died in Quang Tri Province Viet Nam at the age of 21.

How could he get killed? The war in Viet Nam and my own mortality started to hit home. Ray Hodorowski was the epitome of an American Soldier.

At Ray's funeral wake, I heard for the first time a variation on a Bible hymn, modified to fit those times and recited by one of Ray's friends to demonstrate their fearlessness and bravado.

While the Viet Nam War lasted from 1954 to 1975, President Lyndon Johnson - after Kennedy's death - ramped up the war effort. In 1967, there was an astonishing number of U.S. troops stationed in Viet Nam, reportedly more than 500,000 strong. Many young men in my generation were being called up to fight a war in a jungle 8,000 miles away.

I will always remember the saying I heard that day. It struck me as my generation's brave attitude toward facing the possibility of serving in the Viet Nam War:

"Yea, though I walk through the valley of the shadow of death, I will fear no evil; for I am the baddest motherfucker in the valley."

It was a next-man-up and have-no-fear mantra for all those serving and those who would be taking Ray's place. Most of those guys were either heading to or coming back from "the Nam," the terminology used back in the day.

Ray Hodorowski's death introduced me to the Viet Nam War. The death of our friends in the war was an effect felt by my generation. Brave young men like Ray were supposed to be the next generation that would grow up to run this country and dominate the world. Nothing was supposed to be out of reach.

Soon he and other young men would not hear the roar of their car engines at the drag strip but rather the steady "thump, thump, thump" of helicopter blades while they fought an endless war halfway around the world.

The music they heard would no longer be the mellow summer songs by the Beach Boys, but rather the pounding rock of The Rolling Stones and Jimmy Hendrix.

Bob Dylan, known more for his folk songs, penned the famous song, "The Times They Are A-Changin'."

These young warriors of my generation were reflected throughout all of America. They enlisted, volunteered for the draft or were drafted to serve their country.

They wanted to be American Soldiers.

Our military leaders had at their disposal the greatest young warriors ever.

In his book The Beast Was Out There, Brigadier Gen. James E Shelton wrote:

"... in the realm of human conflict, Americans have learned that history teaches two guiding principles:

1. Develop a warrior class within the nation that is part of the nation.

2. Try to avoid armed conflict at all costs but ensure that potential adversaries know that Americans are willing to use their power, if necessary, to defend their vital national interests."

My generation grew up rugged and strong, we competed with and fought with each other, we learned early on how to safely handle weapons and become accomplished marksmen. We believed we would be brave and patriotic if called to serve. Our leaders needed to consider the fighting force they had at their disposal.

Those same leaders needed to follow sound military concepts developed over thousands of years of war, such as applying fundamental guiding principles as reflected in the age-old handbook on war, *The Art of War* by Sun Tzu. He wrote:

"Regard your soldiers as your children, and they will follow you into the deepest valleys; look upon them as your own beloved sons, and they will stand by you even unto death."

At the time, fighting for your country and a just cause was courageous. Our American soldiers would gladly fight bravely and, if necessary, sacrifice their lives.

However, fighting an endless war such as Viet Nam - motivated by what appeared only to be a show of raw power, directed by politicians and fueled primarily to reflect opposition to Communism with the indirect result of massive military profits of the military industrial complex - strained our commitment and contradicted the concept of placing the lives of your soldiers as paramount and reducing the risk of death to a minimum.

And when you include Joe Helmich's manuscript into this equation, where the CIA used the war to cultivate the drug trade to create profits for its black ops, the Viet Nam War makes one skeptical at best as to what was our true mission there.

For many, the war effort only ensured military spending with no clear goal in sight.

It seemed that there had to be a better way to assert our position and the sacrifice of so many of those young men in our generation. The approach and conduct of Viet Nam is not how you get young men to follow you into the "deepest valleys."

I fear during that time some of our leaders - specifically President Johnson and our misguided politicians supported by the military industrial complex - did not look upon these young men as their own beloved sons nor did they have the best interests of our troops at heart in how they prosecuted the Viet Nam War.

There were more than 58,000 mothers during the Viet Nam War who experienced the devastation that Mrs. Hodorowski felt when she was given the news of her son's death. Many other families had sons return who were wounded, physically or mentally, yet these young, brave warriors never received adequate treatment and support once they were back home.

Many of our friends and family members left their hometowns to serve their country. They left with confident attitudes, armed only with pictures of loved ones as they went off to battle in Viet Nam, willing to sacrifice and serve.

Those of us privileged to go to college left our hometowns gladly clutching our football scholarships or deferment papers. Those of us lucky enough left for college knowing that these young warriors from our neighborhoods volunteered to sacrifice their lives for us.

Their military service allowed those of us who went off to college to escape the horror of that war they fought for us, which we were reminded of daily by watching the evening news, and unfortunately, by attending too many funerals.

I will forever be proud of them, but I have always felt a lingering personal guilt for not having served in the military as my brother did, and my father had before him. Many in my generation had those same feelings. That was also my reality during that time.

The Viet Nam War had an immensely negative effect on the psyche of my generation, both for those who served and those who did not, perhaps because the war was pursued with no real purpose or goals that could be explained to our generation. I viewed it as an endless bloody war randomly snatching the lives of our friends. Even worse, the treatment of our American soldiers at the time they returned home was disgraceful.

The military industrial complex profited from that war yet they did not take some of those profits to establish appropriate treatment centers to cope with the physical and mental problems of our returning veterans. They were not lauded as heroes, and in some cases, were subjected to derision. The treatment of our returning soldiers from Viet Nam was as much a tragedy as the war itself and that was preventable. The military industrial complex did not treat these returning veterans as their own beloved sons. The suicide rate of our veterans will forever be a black stain on America.

The wheels of the Viet Nam war rolled for over a decade and left in its tracks the lives of my friends and others in my generation with no satisfactory answer as to why it was really fought and certainly without victory after the tremendous sacrifices made.

Keep all that in mind as you look back at the questions surrounding the Kennedy Assassination in 1963. This was an emotionally taxing time to grow up in America. The exercise of power advocated by the hawkish military industrial complex was designed to address the Soviet aggression in Europe and the expansion of communism into our hemisphere.

There was also a growing communist grip in other parts of the world. Communism was literally 90 miles south of the U.S. in Cuba and on the march. There was much to be concerned about and many in the military industrial complex in America wanted so badly to attack Cuba and other countries to block the spread of communism.

The thought that the sacrifice of our American soldiers fighting was for a noble cause at least comforted the families of the young men who were at risk. The families of those young men could at least cling to the thoughts there was a purpose for their service, and in some cases, their deaths or the disabilities many came home with.

Kennedy never wanted that war to expand the way it had. He was not going to peddle the Viet Nam War as an honorable fight since it was based in large part on the military industrial complex advocating a poorly thought-out military approach. Kennedy had a peaceful vision for our future, but the military industrial complex would not let Kennedy's vision be fulfilled.

CHAPTER 18

The End Of American Idealism

JFK's EFFORTS TO BRING PEACE
TO THE WORLD WERE SHOT DOWN

The assassination of John F. Kennedy signaled the end of that dream of peace and with it, the start of a nightmare that young Americans experienced for the next decade.

Kennedy had his own concept on how to bring peace to a world that was rapidly growing more dangerous, mainly because of something Americans invented and others copied - the atomic bomb. Kennedy did not accept the approach to Cuba being advanced by those in the military industrial complex. If he had, the United States would have invaded Cuba at the start of Castro's takeover.

Kennedy's speech during the Cuban Missile Crisis when faced with the Soviet threat literally 90 miles from Florida stated: "Our goal is not the victory of might, but the vindication of right - not peace at the expense of freedom, but both peace and freedom, here in this hemisphere, and, we hope, around the world."

Hardly a call to arms to attack Cuba. Kennedy would allow co-existence if Castro stopped meddling in politics in other countries in the Western Hemisphere.

It was a trying time. The military and specifically, the CIA, criticized Kennedy for not attacking Cuba. Say what you will about

Kennedy's decision, but we have since learned that former Secretary of Defense Robert McNamara wrote in his memoirs that not only were those Soviet missiles in Cuba armed with nuclear warheads pointed at the Eastern Seaboard of the United States, but the Cuban commanders who controlled those missiles were authorized to call for their launch in the event of an invasion.

Had Kennedy given the signal to launch an all-out attack, we would have had Hiroshima-sized nuclear bombs exploding in retaliation. Close to 150,000 died in Hiroshima. We could have been faced with more massive damage and loss of life from those nuclear weapons raining down on the Eastern Seaboard, launched in response to a full-blown invasion of Cuba.

Kennedy managed to avoid that utter disaster. The military and CIA were not aligned with Kennedy's military posture and felt the lack of war with Cuba was a betrayal of our national interest. Perhaps their anger should have been focused on how our country's intelligence agencies, specifically the CIA, failed us in Cuba, which nearly caused a nuclear tragedy for America, and how they continued to fail us for years thereafter.

The military industrial complex should have looked inward at its own intelligence failures, and they should have been grateful for Kennedy that he made the hard decision to play the hand he was dealt. Instead, they remained at odds. The military industrial complex also had plans for Viet Nam, which did not synchronize with Kennedy's.

These facts forebode troubling times ahead.

I wanted to identify the times we were in from both a historical basis but also from the view of a young man who lived in those times to frame the basis of why an orchestrated coup d'etat by the Deep State was an explainable act. In fact, such a coup d'etat may not have even been considered treasonous by the perpetrators, since they may have justified their actions as necessary and well-reasoned to protect the United States from foreign enemies.

It is not inconceivable to consider that the military industrial complex could justify its acts - removing what it perceived as a weak

President, leading our country down the wrong path.

I am not an apologist for those behind the assassination. I am only pointing out logical facts, when applied with inductive and deductive reasoning as to the times we were in and the actions that were taking place in regard to our Cold War conduct with the Soviet Union, the Bay of Pigs Invasion and the Cuban Missile Crisis under Kennedy's watch.

All of these events were potentially triggering points and reasons for these perpetrators to justify their actions and create regime change in the United States.

I offer Helmich's prearranged transfer of top-secret codes to allow the Soviets to intercept U.S. Military communications on Nov. 22, 1963 as an additional fact to help explain why such a coup d'etat could have taken place.

Add that fact, supported by Helmich's conviction and life sentence for the espionage act, to the tremendous research done by many others on the Kennedy Assassination, and you have yourself one compelling argument to support a coup.

Consider the possible mindset of these powerful men wanting to advance their military objective when you consider the information that Helmich provided me and as written in his *KAK: Manuscript:* some individuals or organizations knew well in advance as to what was planned Nov. 22, 1963. Consider that my client delivered the top-secret military coding equipment and then-current codes to the Soviets so that they could monitor U.S. Military communications after the Kennedy assassination.

By Helmich's delivery of the then-current crypto codes, the Soviets would be able to intercept top-secret communications and know there would be no retaliation on them as an enemy to the United States. Why would such retaliation take place since the military industrial complex knew that the Soviets were not responsible for the assassination?

Helmich himself related that when he met with the Soviets the day after the Kennedy Assassination to deliver the top-secret codes, they indicated they mourned Kennedy's death because he promoted peace. Helmich said the Soviets stated to him directly they believed the CIA backed the assassination.

Recognize that those military leaders and those in charge of our intelligence agencies at the time were tested in world battles and recognized the evils posed by communism. By their experience, they had the badge of justification and claimed patriotism. The growth of communism was occurring throughout the world. This new threat fueled the leaders' views that America needed to be the powerful World Policeman.

There is a distinct line between patriotism and jingoism. Certain of these military leaders and influential individuals in our intelligence community may have fought to defend our country. They may have had the belief that in order to be a patriot you must support America and advocate that America should be exercising its influence and initiate wars to protect our country. But history has taught us that most wars were initiated by tyrants. These individuals may also have justified their actions by their belief that Kennedy was not protecting what they had fought so very hard to achieve years before he took office.

They may have believed that Kennedy's actions in attempting to secure world peace rather than encouraging new wars somehow itself was a threat to the America that they fought for. This is not to condone what they did, rather to point out another logical basis why a coup d'etat by the military industrial complex or Deep State could have occurred in America due to extreme patriots crossing over the line of patriotism to jingoism.

Let us use inductive and deductive reasoning. One must consider the facts that we know existed and apply them logically to arrive at the correct explanation rather than injecting unknown issues which would increase the chances for an erroneous result.

For example, rather than apply the bizarre and complex pretzel logic analysis used by the Warren Commission to explain what happened by forcing the theory of an isolated, lone-wolf gunman in Lee Harvey Oswald, simply consider what any fundamental analysis of a major crime requires: Identification of Means, Motive and Opportunity.

As applied to the information on the Kennedy Assassination, the facts lead to the conclusion that:

1. A stealth and experienced CIA-controlled hit squad could have been given the necessary weaponry and inside information (Means) on the target location. With tacit cooperation or directions to Kennedy's protective services to stand down or relax their protection, the door was opened to allow the assassination to take place.

2. A group of powerful individuals had the Motive, whether correct or not, to take it upon themselves to eliminate the leader of this country who they believed posed a clear and present danger to national security.

3. It was predetermined that the target, here Kennedy, would be at his most vulnerable as his motorcade travelled through Dealey Plaza at a snail's pace (average 11 mph) giving the shooter - or shooters - the opportunity for the kill shot.

Means, Motive and Opportunity were present for an orchestrated assassination of Kennedy in Dallas on Nov. 22, 1963. The facts support that conclusion, hard as it would have been to accept it at the time or perhaps to even believe it now.

Analytically and without emotion, once you overcome the shock or disbelief that someone or some organization in our country could actually undertake this, the conspiracy set up to assassinate Kennedy is absolutely more rational to accept than the explanation of the wildly exotic tale the Warren Commission spun.

To further dismiss the findings in the Warren Commission Report, consider the implausible post-death actions that occurred, which included taking Kennedy's body out of Dallas, the scene of the murder, to have an autopsy performed by an unqualified doctor in Washington D.C. who had never performed an autopsy on a shooting victim.

A rational overview of the extremely odd behavior post-death of all the governmental agencies points to bewildering conduct on the part of our government, to say the least. Or damning conduct dependent on your viewpoint.

Look objectively at the handling of the evidence. Compound that with the numerous propped-up assumptions of the Warren Commission. Keep in mind that Allen Dulles was the head of the CIA before being fired by Kennedy in 1961 after the Bay of Pigs disaster. Dulles then later served on the Warren Commission. No better fox-guarding-the-henhouse analogy can be made.

The Warren Commission advanced the wholly unbelievable Single Bullet Theory to create evidence to support their assassination theory. With each year that passes and with more information being revealed, there is a growing number of Americans that do not accept the Warren Commission's findings. More than half of Americans don't believe the report and only a small minority of Americans believe Oswald acted alone.

The assumptions in the Warren Report were introduced in a design to rearrange facts and evidence to support a single-gunman theory, essentially to rewrite history.

Look at the way the evidence was mishandled. Again, being objective, it would be hard to reconcile that the prosecution at a murder trial could ever have convicted Oswald of the assassination since much of the evidence would have been inadmissible or tainted based upon the chain of custody just off the "Magic Bullet" alone.

As more information has been revealed, such as the detailed analysis by Oliver Stone in his movie *JFK: Revisited*, and many others who have spent literally their entire lives devoted to ferret out the truth on the assassination, it is astounding as to the mountain of evidence that was mishandled, altered or overlooked. This significant amount of evidence that has been compiled leads to the inescapable conclusion that this was a coup d'etat run by the Deep State, not some random act by a lone gunman with no motivation like Lee Harvey Oswald who professed he was a "patsy" before his own murder.

Look at the evidence as an attorney would or a Trier of Fact viewing the evidence. In doing so you will recognize that much was being covered up and none of the evidence advocated to be the true facts leads you to the conclusion the Warren Commission wanted you to accept.

By Executive Order, President Lyndon Johnson established the President's Commission on the Assassination of President Kennedy on Nov. 29, 1963.

An 888-page final report was presented to President Johnson on Sept. 24, 1964. After he read and edited it, it was made public three days later.

In my opinion, the goal of the Warren Commission was not to establish evidence to convict Oswald or present the truth at trial. The objective view is that its goal was to have a safe explanation for this tragedy. It pinned its findings on happenstance and a lone wolf gunman rather than the reality that this was the removal of the President from within and a regime change by the Deep State in America.

The actions were done to placate the bereaved public. In doing so they would announce this conclusion of a lone-wolf gunman by a blue-ribbon panel hand selected to arrive at a predetermined conclusion. The Warren Commission Report also took the spotlight off the actual planners of the coup d'etat. Note there also was a plan in place to eliminate Oswald so that he could never see the inside of a courtroom to tell his side of the story.

Much like many of the exhaustive studies done on witnesses to the Kennedy Assassination. There were many people who spent countless hours of their time analyzing the possible testimony of more than 100 people who died strange or unusual deaths.

What are the mathematical odds of more than 100 deaths out of the group of all those potential witnesses? A billion to one! Many of those deaths occurred just before the witness was to testify. Apply Occam's razor problem solving analysis format and inductive and deductive reasoning to those statistics to form the inescapable conclusion that these deaths were not natural or accidental.

The truth could never be revealed. The American people at the time would never accept a seizure of power by a group of powerful individuals in the United States regardless of the justification claimed.

Nor would that powerful group allow the American public to even consider that this was a staged event. On a regular basis, coup d'états were happening in other countries. In fact, a coup d'etat took place in Viet Nam just weeks before.

On Nov. 1, a coup led by General Duon Van Minh deposed President Ngo Dinh Diem and the Personalist Labor Revolutionary Party of the Republic of Viet Nam. Reports years later said the CIA backed the operation. The captured Diem was executed the next day, along with his brother.

Other coups took place in Central and South America, Africa and elsewhere at the time, thanks to the CIA. The CIA specialized in regime change throughout the world. Clearly with the right conditions, this could, and I suggest did happen in America. The CIA's fingerprints are all over this assassination or at least, it seemed the CIA was aware, in advance, of the plans to remove Kennedy. Whether it was the CIA or some other organization, Helmich's assignment was planned well in advance to occur directly after Kennedy's assassination.

The conventional wisdom was that the American people would accept the fairy tale that the Warren Commission created for the good of the country, rather than the logical explanation that the facts supported.

The "Bigger Lie" theory was presented because that fit the narrative of the Deep State. Oswald, the apparent lone gunman, lived long enough to announce that he was a patsy.

Hardly the message a crazed lone gunman would announce since there had to be a motivation for the act. But as in all conspiracies, it is important to eliminate all the witnesses. The American public is smart and perceptive. That is why after all of those investigations and attempted explanations, the majority of Americans still believe that Kennedy's assassination was due to a conspiracy. And that number of skeptical citizens grew a decade later.

When Gallup conducted a poll from Nov. 22-27, 1963, it found that 29 percent of Americans believed one man was responsible for the shooting and 52 percent believed others were involved in a conspiracy. By 1976, Americans' belief in the conspiracy theory swelled to 81 percent.

Helmich's manuscript pointed to just one part of a well-planned plot. The facts involving the turnover by Helmich of top-secret codes on the day of the Kennedy Assassination supported the position that there was at least one organization, perhaps more, that knew of the event well in advance.

That meant there was a conspiracy to assassinate President Kennedy since it certainly involved more than one person and there was knowledge of the event in advance. My interview with Helmich that summer day in Talladega and his manuscript opened my eyes to the events that led to Kennedy's assassination.

It was another piece of the massive collection of evidence to support the reason why some organizations felt that this tragedy would be in our national interest. Name it the Deep State for ease of reference. It doesn't matter: Tremendous evil was on display in the United States on Friday, Nov. 22, 1963.

Helmich's transfer of our top military codes to the Soviets the day after the Kennedy assassination is evidence that needs to be shared with others who have thoughtfully tracked or unearthed the treasure trove of other evidence questioning the Kennedy Assassination.

The Oscar-winning film *JFK* implied that President Lyndon Johnson may have been involved in such a conspiracy.

As to the Johnson presidency and looking back on these events, a song that reminds me of that time following Kennedy's assassination and specifically what I observed happen to our society directly afterwards, is the song "The End of the Innocence" by Don Henley.

The lyrics vividly describe beautiful skies that turn dark, and how society quickly devolves to the whims of a king.

This song confirmed to me what I felt when I first learned of the Kennedy Assassination and then later as I saw the Viet Nam War develop and unfold. The Viet Nam War soon became a reality of our country, bringing death to countless family friends and others from my generation.

Henley may have penned that beautiful and reflective song in part about President Ronald Reagan, but for me it will always be directed to Lyndon Johnson, who reversed Kennedy's course on Viet Nam before Kennedy's body was in the grave.

"The End of the Innocence" seems especially poignant to the events I describe in this book.

Johson's actions alone answer the question of "Why?" as to the Kennedy Assassination. The answer was to green light a full-blown war effort in Southeast Asia.

A massive investment in weaponry. Great business for arms dealers, weapons dealers, plane and vehicle makers, oil companies and those who supplied food, all accomplices of the military industrial complex. The objective facts are that there was a major direction change in our foreign policy in Southeast Asia immediately after the assassination.

On Nov. 26, 1963 - one day after President Kennedy's funeral - President Johnson approved National Security Action Memorandum 273. Also called NSAM-273, it resulted from the need to reassess U.S. policy toward the Viet Nam War after the overthrow and assassination of President Diem.

The result of that foreign policy direction change: massive profits being made from the war effort due to a significant ramp up in military spending. The real cost to make those profits for the war machine was the blood of our country's sons, the American Soldiers.

From the facts I have assembled I am convinced that the Viet Nam War would not have been conducted in the way it was had Kennedy lived. Kennedy's Assassination and the Viet Nam War was The End of American Idealism.

CHAPTER 19

The Heroic
American Soldier

WE OWE A DEBT OF GRATITUDE
TO ALL WHO HAVE DEFENDED FREEDOM

When I hear Bruce Springsteen's "Born in the USA" lyrics, about a brother fighting off the Viet Cong, it instantly reminds me of my brother. I am thankful that Army Spec. 5 Kenneth A. Jursinski - who served at An Khe Province in the Central Highlands of Viet Nam - returned safely.

My brother Ken volunteered for the draft. He went to Germany on a choice assignment where he could have remained during the Viet Nam War before likely returning home safely. My brother, however, volunteered to go to Viet Nam in hopes of meeting up with his longtime friend, Bob Nagy. Bob and my brother together volunteered for the draft on the same day. Unlike my brother, Bob was assigned to fight in Viet Nam. Ken Jursinski was an American Soldier.

A Family Tradition

Ken followed in the footsteps of our father, who was a captain in the U.S. Army, and was a battle-tested and wounded veteran who fought in arguably the bloodiest and most pivotal battle in World

War II, the Battle of the Bulge. It was fought in and around Bastogne, Belgium and the Ardennes Forest.

For the 60th anniversary of the Battle of the Bulge, I took my wife Darlene and my three daughters Jamie, Lauren and Kara, to visit Bastogne and LaRoche, Belgium, which was in close proximity to Bastogne. My father boldly led his company of soldiers, fought and returned home alive.

I kept in contact with a wonderful elderly woman who knew my father when he was stationed near LaRoche. Her name was Giselle and at the time of the war she was the daughter of the mayor of LaRoche during WWII. We met her and she recalled that my father helped the beleaguered and starving residents of LaRoche by supplying food and supplies while, at the same time, being in charge of his own company of soldiers.

We also met the mayor of LaRoche. My entire family and I were treated like royalty. As a show of gratitude, we were guests at a seven-course dinner at the local castle in LaRoche on Bastille Day. This was a way for the town of LaRoche to express their gratitude for what my father and his fellow soldiers did for the citizens of LaRoche more than 60 years before.

My dad never spoke about the Battle of the Bulge to me. We saw pictures of his blown-up Jeep and photos of my dad with bandages on his face after he was wounded. My dad never talked about the war or said much of anything about what he did in the bloodiest battle of World War II.

I learned more from speaking with Gisele and other older citizens of Laroche about what he did than what my dad had told me. My dad was brave and very kind to those residents of LaRoche and always exhibited that same kindness to his family and friends until the day he died.

Before we left LaRoche, we stopped at Gisele's home. As we left her home knowing it was unlikely we would ever see her again, I recall that Gisele opened a cabinet drawer, pulled out a lace handkerchief, unfolded it and disclosed my father's Captain's bars. Gisele kept those Captain's bars all those years. With a tear in her eye and a smile on her face she handed them to me and gave me a big hug. My dad, U.S. Army Captain Frank "Jay" Jursinski was an American Soldier.

We left LaRoche to travel the farm fields bordering the Ardennes's Forest where the Battle of the Bulge raged. Hard to imagine 400,000 German troops supported by Panzer tank brigades rolling over those hills in attack formation. An American Soldier would have needed to have the heart of a lion to have the courage to stand up to that attack.

We located an area close to where we believe my wife's uncle, Army Sergeant Bernard Deem fought. Bernard was a member of the 193rd Glider Infantry Regiment, an airborne infantry regiment during World War II and part of the 17th Airborne Division that fought during the Battle of the Bulge.

Darlene's uncle and my father did not know cach other but they both fought bravely in the same epic battle. Sergeant Bernard Deem of Parkersburg, West Virginia, unlike my father, did not return home but was killed during the Battle of the Bulge. Bernard's Mom had to receive the heartbreaking news that she would never again see her oldest son. Mrs. Deem had to live with that thought each night as she cried herself to sleep. Sergeant Bernard Deem was an American Soldier.

Several days later, we travelled to my dad's parents and my grandparents' original home area outside of Krakow, Poland. About an hour's drive from the Krakow area where they grew up was the Auschwitz concentration camp. Walking those streets, entering those buildings at Auschwitz and seeing the utter inhumanity of man in that death camp made it black and white why my dad and all the other American Soldiers fought in World War II.

The mission of the Viet Nam War was not as clear. I still cannot reconcile the national interest at stake in Viet Nam with the comparison to the death camp in Auschwitz. I will always regard with contempt President Lydon Johnson and the other politicians responsible for Viet Nam and the way they orchestrated that endless war with no true national interest identified and with nothing achieved except the sacrifice of blood and treasure and more directly, the death of young men of my generation.

Honoring Their Bravery And Sacrifice

Like many other childhood friends, Bob Nagy never returned. Bob's story and that of his Battalion, and others from my hometown of Lorain, Ohio, deserve further mention due to their heroism and sacrificing their lives.

Bob Nagy was a badass. He was an Army Private First Class (PFC) in the third Platoon, Company D, 2nd Battalion of the 28th Infantry Regiment of the U.S. Army.

The 28th Infantry Regiment, known as the Black Lions, was a historic and distinguished unit in the United States Army. The Black Lions have participated in many significant events throughout U.S. Military history.

The Black Lions fought in the infamous Battle of Ong Thanh in Binh Long Province, Viet Nam. In October 1967, the Black Lions were ambushed and soundly defeated by the 271st Regiment of the 9th Viet Cong Division in the Battle of Ong Thanh.

The ambush of the Black Lions took place in an isolated and dense jungle area. That bloody battle was the subject of a book by the late Gen. James E. Shelton, ominously titled *The Beast Was Out There.*

Bob Nagy was killed on Oct. 17, 1967, in the Battle of Ong Thanh. He was 20 years old. Bob Nagy was an American Soldier.

I cried as I read Bob's name etched in stone at the Viet Nam Memorial in Washington, D.C. Other friends and warriors from Lorain whose names I also read cut into those black granite slabs at the Memorial: Marines Ronnie Ralich and Ray Hodorowski along with 96 other soldiers from Lorain County that died in Viet Nam.

PFC Ronnie Ralich, a rifleman in the Marine Corps, served in G Company, 2nd Battalion, 1st Marines, 1st Marine Division. In his final mission, on May 29, 1966, Ronnie was part of Golf Platoon. A large group of NVA soldiers in an area called Thua Thien Viet Nam set up a horseshoe ambush for Ronnie and Golf Platoon members.

Ronnie Ralich, just 19, was one of 20 Marines and a corpsman killed in that battle. The battle Ronnie fought in was documented in a book titled *The Ghosts of Thua Thien: An American Soldier's Memoir of Vietnam* by John A. Nesser. Ronnie is one of those Ghosts of Thua Thien. Ronnie Ralich was an American Soldier.

In the Fall of 1965, while I was a sophomore in high school at Lorain St. Mary's, it was announced that a former distinguished student was killed in Viet Nam. His name was Don Bonko.

Don Bonko was voted All-Ohio as halfback his senior year in high school. He was an excellent student as well as an athlete. Don attended the U.S. Military Academy at West Point, lettering on the 1958 Army football team that went undefeated.

After graduating, Don went on to serve as captain in the U.S. Army in Viet Nam and was part of the 1st Infantry Division, called the *Big Red One.* Bob Nagy's Black Lions were also part of the *Big Red One.*

Don was awarded the Bronze Star, Purple Heart and Combat Infantryman's Badge. He was 28 years old when he was killed on Nov. 26, 1965 while on a mission. Don Bonko was an American Soldier.

Don, and so many others during that time, were among the best and brightest. He gave his life willingly for his country during the ramp up of the war encouraged by President Lyndon Johnson.

Hero Behind The Heisman

In my freshman year at Akron in the fall of 1968 I was on one of the best football teams ever at Akron, which had a rich history of football. John Heisman, after whom the Heisman Trophy was named, was the first paid football coach at Akron.

Many years later while I was a modestly successful NFL agent representing a number of NFL players, I was selected to represent the family of Frank Eliscu, considered by many to be America's greatest sculptor. One of his iconic works is the massive five story frieze sculpture that sits atop the doors of the Library of Congress in Washington D.C. The other famous work Frank designed and created was the Heisman Memorial Football Trophy in 1935 when he was only 23 years old. He was paid the grand total of $33 for the licensing rights to the original sculptor by the Downtown New York Athletic Club.

Frank retained the original statue and bequeathed it to his daughter, Norma. She retained me to assist her when she wanted to sell off the original Heisman Trophy. I am one of the few people in America who has held the original Heisman Trophy. It was an amazing thrill when I first saw this original sculpture, considered the most iconic individual trophy in America.

In 2005 we successfully auctioned off the original Heisman Trophy in New York City with the sale being conducted by Sotheby's. The original Heisman statue sold for $240,000. The Eliscu family thanked me for my work and gave me an original Frank Eliscu statue, *Daniel in the Lion's Den*. They also gave me an original silver medallion created by Mr. Eliscu for the Commercial Litigation society. Frank Eliscu was not only one of America's greatest sculptors, he served in the U.S. Army during World War II. Frank Eliscu was an American Soldier.

All Veterans Deserve Our Gratitude

All of those who volunteered to serve or were called to serve did so believing that there was national interest at stake, and they needed to protect that interest.

We enjoy our lives of freedom in America because of young men like Bob Nagy, Ronnie Ralich, Ray Hodorowski and Don Bonko, as well as the sacrifices of all those who served.

My firm belief is that their sacrifice may not have been required if Kennedy himself had lived. Viet Nam would not have happened, certainly not in the scope or manner it evolved, had Kennedy not been assassinated.

To have a Viet Nam War, the Deep State needed to eliminate John Fitzgerald Kennedy.

Joseph Helmich survived but he saw his own horrors when transferred to Saigon as part of the U.S. Army Security Agency. He told me of an aborted attempt on his life after an internal dispute with a number of those involved in the storing and transporting of the heroin that Helmich wrote was being exported under the direction of the CIA.

In a *United Press International* story, Helmich had photos of men who had their heads blown off during the war.

All of the young men who fought in Viet Nam - and all of the young men and women who have defended freedom before and after Viet Nam - are American Soldiers. These warriors were beautifully memorialized in the lyrics of the Toby Keith song, "American Soldier."

Keith's lyrics strikingly honor the courage of the American Soldier. He proudly describes how steadfast American Soldiers stand in harm's way, and how they are willing to stay in the fight at all costs to defend freedom, even if that means they must make the ultimate sacrifice.

Also, as stated by one of Ronnie Ralich's friends on his memorial page to all of those American Soldiers who gave the ultimate sacrifice: "Rest in the heavens Warriors"

We owe it to all those who sacrificed, as well as to ourselves, to recognize what is taking place in our country and stand up for our beliefs. Each and every one of us need to be that one voice that supports and elects leaders who have the morality to use the power they have been entrusted wisely and with responsibility, and certainly not for personal gain.

We should defend the United States of America for honor's sake and for our national interests. We should not prosecute endless wars solely to generate profits for the war machine.

GROWING UP

CHAPTER 20

Growing Up In America

LIVING WITH THE THREAT OF NUCLEAR WAR
AND DEADLY CHILDHOOD DISEASES

My generation - the Baby Boomers - had the pride of growing up in the greatest and most powerful country in the world in the 1950s and 1960s. The designation "Baby Boomers" was applied to children born from approximately 1946 through 1964. The term "Boomer" was applied since there was a tidal wave of births and growth of families after World War II.

While children born during this time period grew up in the most powerful country on Earth, Baby Boomers had to deal with a number of threats. One overarching threat was a nuclear attack and the anxiety of the Cold War.

While President Kennedy started his first years in office and handled crisis after crisis, such as the Cuban Missile Crisis, Special Warrant Officer Joseph G. Helmich deciphered codes in the secured block house in Paris. He recognized that America and the Soviet Union were on the brink of nuclear war.

During those times in the early 1960s, students of my generation regularly participated in duck-and-cover drills in school, simulating protective actions to take in the event of a nuclear bomb blast. The official government video identified the duck-and-cover technique as if hiding under your school desk would protect one from a nuclear blast.

While intended to provide protection, the drills were criticized for their limited effectiveness in a real nuclear attack, as they did not address the long-term dangers of radiation exposure or the potential for widespread destruction.

In addition to the drills at school, many families built personal fallout shelters in their basements, stocking them with food and supplies to survive the aftermath of a nuclear attack. I am not sure what Floridians did since they did not have basements, but it was certainly a common practice to store food and be prepared for a nuclear attack.

In Florida, the state's civil defense department designated businesses, hotels and hospitals as fallout shelters.

My generation had the constant fear of nuclear war hanging over our heads like the Sword of Damocles, ready to destroy our population in an instant. This ongoing threat created a level of fear and anxiety for all citizens of America. We heard the warning, accepted that reality and continued with our lives and studies. We were resilient.

In addition to the threat of nuclear attack, Baby Boomers dealt with life-threatening diseases. Among the most merciless killer diseases affecting children were scarlet fever, diphtheria, typhoid fever, yellow fever, rheumatic fever, pellagra, influenza and smallpox. As late as the 1950s, children died of measles or whooping cough.

In the 1950s, polio was one of the deadliest deadly childhood diseases in the United States, causing thousands of deaths and lifelong disabilities. Polio attacked the central nervous system, causing partial or full paralysis. Many survivors faced lifelong consequences, such as deformed limbs, the need for crutches, wheelchairs or breathing devices.

It was reported that polio epidemics in America occurred each summer in at least one part of the country. Polio was transmitted from fecal matter and there was a school of thought that the polio virus was transmitted when children swam in pools or lakes. Polio was a relentless and evil disease waiting to kill or paralyze some of America's children.

The worst recorded U.S. outbreak of polio was in 1952, with over 3,000 deaths and countless disabilities among children. It could cause flu-like symptoms, but it could also affect the brain and spinal cord, leading to meningitis and paralysis. All of those children in my generation growing up in that era had to deal with that threat. It was ever present.

Thankfully, effective vaccines introduced by Dr. Jonas Salk largely eliminated the fear of polio in the United States. A separate vaccine developed in 1961 by Albert Sabin effectively eradicated this horrible disease that attacked children. The vaccine however did not eliminate the disease entirely and in certain circumstances, the reaction to the vaccine itself brought on the disease or symptoms of polio.

My experience with polio came from one of my classmates who was afflicted with the disease at my Catholic grade school, Nativity of the Blessed Virgin Mary.

My friend and classmate's name was Eddie Romanski. He contracted polio at an early age. I recall that he wore heavy leg braces and could not play with us at recess. Over the course of some years, Eddie showed some improvement, but then relapsed.

I recall that his wonderful mother brought him to school, picked him up and oftentimes monitored him during the day. It was a full-time job. She always tried to smile, but even at my young age, I could tell her son's condition was tearing her apart. You could see the strain on her face and the dark circles under her eyes. She had the constant worry of watching her son suffer from this cruel monster of a disease. She wore a mask of grief. Eddie's mom was also a victim of this merciless disease.

Eddie's mom tried to normalize his life, including having me and some other classmates come to his house for a birthday party and sleepover trying to make all of us happy as she worried about her son. It is hard to imagine what she had to go through, since she suffered right along with Eddie.

That all would come to an end. Eddie died in the seventh grade. I was a pallbearer at his funeral along with some of my classmates. We carried his polio riddled body from the church to the hearse and then to the burial plot at Calvary Cemetery in Lorain. I watched his mother as Eddie was put to rest that day. It was painful to see her face as the tears rolled down her cheeks. A mother should not have to bury her son. A 12-year-old should not have to be a pallbearer for a childhood friend.

That was my first experience with death. I would have a short reprieve for a few more years before I started attending funerals for other childhood friends killed in Viet Nam. I continued to see that same utter sadness and grief on the faces of fallen soldiers' mothers.

These women, like countless mothers across America, had to live through the horror of America's sons being brought home in body bags from the war in Viet Nam that President Johnson delivered to us. A war seemingly with no end or purpose.

I didn't know this at the time, but while my friend Eddie was dying from polio, a young girl in Springfield, Ohio was herself battling polio. She contracted the disease as a reaction to the polio vaccine. The medical term for this is vaccine-associated paralytic polio. Simplistically, the vaccine injected into a child reproduces in the intestine and can revert to a neurovirulent strain that causes polio. Vaccines to prevent diseases such as polio save lives but there are consequences to certain people from the vaccine. The reaction to the polio vaccine was present in a small percentage of the population.

In 2025, the concern over vaccines remained at the forefront thanks to Robert F. Kennedy, Jr., the Health And Human Services Secretary for the United States, who advocated a study on the number of vaccines given to our children and the potential linkage to reactions to such vaccines, such as the dramatic increase in childhood autism. Kennedy has advocated studies on the impact of other vaccines, such as the forced vaccines on children from the COVID-19 virus when the statistics reflect that, according to a report from the Mayo Clinic, from 2020 to the end of March 2024, children up to age 17 accounted for only about 1.5 percent of people who needed to be treated for COVID-19.

Kennedy's position is to fully review the effects of all childhood vaccines and find whether there is any linkage to reactive responses, such as the growth of autism in children. Kennedy pointed to statistics that showed in the United States in the 1970s, fewer than three in 10,000 children had autism.

In 2020, the Centers for Disease Control and Prevention estimates that 1 in 150 children eight years of age in the U.S. have autism spectrum disorder (ASD), a staggering increase. Kennedy points out this astonishing increase and wants more studies to determine if there is a link to childhood vaccines.

The young girl from Springfield who contracted polio after taking the vaccine luckily survived. Unlike many children who reacted negatively and died or had lifetime issues with polio, this brave young girl not only fought this horrible disease and recovered, but she went on to lead a healthy life, became a great student and was named captain of her cheerleading squad at Springfield North High School.

Newsweek, in its 50th Anniversary Edition, devoted a large part of its issue to an in-depth report on Springfield, Ohio as the personification of middle America with the city's highs and lows. The Springfield North High cheerleading squad was featured in that issue.

That courageous young girl who battled and beat polio had her picture taken along with her cheerleading teammates featured in Newsweek's 50th Anniversary Edition.

At Kent State, I had the chance to meet that beautiful young cheerleader, Darlene Deem. I ultimately married Darlene, the best decision I ever made in my life.

CHAPTER 21

The Viet Nam Draft Lottery

MY BROTHER'S SELFLESS ACT AND MY FOOLISH
MISTAKES WHICH HAD ME HEADED FOR WAR

In the 1960s and 1970s, Bad Kissingen, Germany was a town known for its spas, drinking culture and beautiful women. Not a bad place to vacation, let alone a place to serve out your military service vs. the deadly jungles of Viet Nam.

So when my brother Ken volunteered to transfer from Bad Kissingen to Viet Nam, he needed to make several requests and required psychological tests.

His commanding officer questioned why he would want to change from a cushy assignment. After Ken continued to insist on a transfer, it was ultimately granted. My brother ended up being stationed at Camp Radcliff outside of An Khe in the Central Highlands of Viet Nam in a combat group.

By volunteering, my brother took the place of another soldier who would have been in his spot in Viet Nam. He didn't know it at the time, but his selfless act in part may have saved me from going to Viet Nam. Because of what my brother did, I had to work through some guilt.

To explain that fully, it's necessary to identify what took place in America with the Viet Nam draft lottery starting my sophomore year at the University of Akron. My own undoing led me to being drafted and inducted into the U.S. Army.

Draft Lottery

As of 1969, there had been no draft in America in the preceding 27 years. The previous draft was in 1942. Since then, America had sufficient volunteers to staff its army.

However, President Johnson's continuing ramp up of the Viet Nam War required more than 500,00 soldiers, far more than were volunteering. His successor, President Richard Nixon, inherited the ramp up. Remember, this war started in 1954.

The Viet Nam War received a lot of scrutiny for having dragged on for five years with no discernible results and mounting national criticism. As such, it became necessary to implement a draft of eligible young men between the ages of 18 to 24 years of age.

The governmental agency that oversaw the draft was the Selective Service System (SSS). The SSS is a federal agency that maintains a database of male U.S. citizens and male immigrants who are potentially subject to military conscription. Note: Women were encouraged to serve in the military and many did, but they were not subject to the draft at that time.

The selection process for the draft lottery resembled gambling lotteries that you see run by states. The SSS draft lottery selection process involved a container of 366 capsules, each capsule containing a specific day of the year and one capsule for Feb 29, leap year. Each capsule was drawn, just like a gambling lottery, and then each birth date was assigned a draft number in sequential order. This draft lottery determined the fate of young men in America who were in the draft pool.

In 1969, the first capsule drawn reflected the date of Sept. 14, 1969. This meant that all men between the ages of 18 and 24 born on Sept. 14 would be called up first, followed by the next capsule reflecting the next birth date and so on.

There also was a secondary phase of the draft lottery, so not only was it a number but it was also your initial. In that way, men born on the same date would be identified in sequential order based upon each of the 26 letters of the alphabet in the order drawn. Your birthdate was assigned a number and your last name, middle initial and first name determined the order of selection for that birthdate. In the first draft, the first alphabet letter drawn was the letter "J" so if your last name started with a "J" like mine, you were the first to be called for that particular birthdate.

For example, an individual by the name of Charles Brett Jones, born on Sept. 14 would be identified as "JBC" as his call name and #1 as the draft number. Accordingly for the 1969 draft, Charles Brett Jones, born on Sept. 14 and between the ages of 18 to 24 translated to "JBC #1." If you were the hypothetical Charles Brett Jones born on Sept 14, or born on Sept 14 regardless of your last name, had no deferment and were able to pass the Army physical you might as well start getting sized up for your jungle boots and combat fatigues.

My birth date is Sept. 22, which was #160 in the call-up rotation of the total of 195 numbers that were being used. My call-up name was a reverse of the initials of first, middle and last name: Kevin Francis Jursinski. So, for the 1969 draft, I was "JFK #160."

Given the fact that there would be 195 numbers called, I knew that without a deferment, "JFK #160" would be one of the first ones called up, headed to the U.S. Army and most likely, Viet Nam.

Good Start, Bad Finish

Lucky for me, all I had to do was maintain a 2.0 grade point average at the University of Akron to keep my deferment and my full-ride football scholarship in place. A 2.0 grade average seemed to be a ridiculously easy goal for me to achieve.

I started at the University of Akron on the dean's list (GPA in excess of 3.5) and had always been a good student. I started high school by finishing in the upper 99th percentile of freshmen upon standardized entrance tests given at the time. Grades came easy for me.

I never had one grade below a "B or a 3.0" at any point in time during grade school or high school and generally had outstanding grades. It seemed a lock for me to maintain a grade point average above a 2.0 to maintain my deferment and my scholarship.

In my first year at Akron, I enrolled in the United States Air Force Reserve Officer Training program (ROTC), with the goal of becoming an officer in the U.S. Air Force. My thought process was that if I did serve with Viet Nam still raging, I wanted to fly over jungles rather than walk through them. By the time I started at Akron, I experienced the death of a number of friends already killed in jungle combat in Viet Nam and I wanted to select a branch of the military I would serve.

The overall goal for me - and every other young man in America with a college deferment - was simple: Study and stay in school.

Keeping my grades up also kept me eligible to play football. I knew that badass or not, a bullet shot from a sniper position or in combat in Viet Nam could have your name on it.

Then came the turning point for me in maintaining my 2.0 grade point average: I pledged to a fraternity – Lambda Chi Alpha – early in my freshman year.

Members of Akron's football and basketball team also pledged. This was a great bunch of guys who all liked to party like me. I had good friends in my pledge class since we were already teammates on the football team. The annual fraternity picture outside of an old-time burlesque/strip club reflected our priorities.

The fraternity route sounded like a great idea. Fraternity parties, fellowship with some great guys and the opportunity to meet sorority girls at mixers.

I was well liked in the fraternity and among the members of my pledge class. I ended up being the leader during *Hell Week* and given the honorary title of the "Jap." Most of my old friends from Akron still call me "Jap," which is actually a sign of respect since it signifies the leader of the pledge class and the person who was the target of the most abuse during *Hell Week*.

We had a number of military veterans in the fraternity and they contributed to the hazing rituals, somewhat similar to boot camp. "Drop and give me 20 (or 40)," was often heard during the pledge period along with other physical training events. We had other hazing rituals in *Hell Week*, many of which were grueling and some downright nasty, bordering on sadistic, including "King Hot Pepper" and the "Fireman's Smoke Inhalation Drill." There was also the overarching technique to breaking the human spirit: Sleep deprivation.

The record for sleep deprivation is 11 days and 25 minutes according to the Guinness Book of World Records. That record never will be broken since Guinness eliminated this category due to the tremendous health danger of sleep deprivation. I can attest that staying up for seven straight days and nights while also being harassed constantly by the active members has an effect on your physical and mental health.

I went from waking up Sunday morning to start *Hell Week* to Saturday night without sleep. I was the only pledge class member that never slept.

I never want to do that again. I am not sure that they do this in U.S. Army basic training, but at the time Army Special Forces, including units like Green Berets, used sleep deprivation as a training tool to a certain extent.

I was also elected Scholarship Chairman by my fraternity, which consisted of more than 100 active members. My brothers put their faith in me because I had one of the highest grade point averages in the fraternity.

My job as Scholarship Chairman was to make sure that everyone maintained their grades to stay in school and remain on their respective varsity teams. This was also important to those fraternity members whose draft numbers were from 1 through 195, since dropping below a 2.0 average meant you also were now eligible for the draft. This was top of mind to every draft eligible young man in the country attending college on a deferment.

Getting drafted in 1969-1970 meant your odds were great on being sent to Viet Nam. Most young men that did not volunteer for the draft or enlist did not want to experience four years in the military and a tour in Viet Nam.

I did a great job at protecting everyone else's grade point average — except my own. My grades suffered after I moved into the fraternity house because every day, one or more of the brothers would come to the house and want to go out at night.

Of course, that meant I was always asked to join in. I ended up partying on a regular basis with a rotation of brothers since I did not have the discipline or interest to focus on my own studies. I cut corners and thought I could get by on doing a quick review of my textbook before the final exam.

I also took a job bartending three nights a week at the Draught House, the largest nightclub in the area for college entertainment. Besides serving drinks (3.2 percent beer) to those 18 and over, there was a high percentage of single women. This regimen resulted in my focus being on girls and partying. As any young man in America at the time can attest, risking your deferment was a dangerous thing with the deadly Viet Nam War raging. That did not phase me.

In addition, I was elected Rush Chairman for the fraternity, which meant I was essentially in charge of recruiting new members by setting up Rush parties. That meant making sure the future pledges to the fraternity had a great time at our house at 94 Fir Hill in Akron, right off campus.

My job was to give future pledges a few drinks and meet a sorority girl or townie. The fraternity's official position to the college administration that no drinking was occurring at the frat house. Of course that was absolutely not the case since we had a bar in the basement of the frat house.

I was a liaison to all the sororities meeting their active members and their own sorority pledge classes. I was in charge of making sure we had plenty of eligible attractive ladies at the Rush parties and plenty of drinks. The Rush Chairman was a job with benefits since I was able to meet a large portion of the young ladies on campus.

I was always a hard worker and did a great job in my position. I worked very hard at partying. Predictably, by partying and bartending, my grades plummeted.

I needed to make money for tuition, room and board since my immaturity during the second quarter also resulted in my decision to forfeit my full-ride football scholarship. That decision still haunts me as the worst decision in my life, made the Monday after Hell Week. Perhaps sleep deprivation for a full week affected my decision. One I still truly regret and think about to this day.

I was given a great opportunity by the coaching staff for whom I have nothing but praise. I performed well but made the decision to leave the team. When I did, it put financial pressure on my parents who already were under a lot of stress. My actions had consequences. To continue in school the following year, I needed to make money to pay for the school year. The consequences of my decision to leave the team was that I had to leave the state and work in Alaska the following summer.

For that Alaska job at Prudhoe Bay, once you reported you had to stay for your full tour assignment. No quitting unless you wanted to walk home.

Taking this job meant I missed several weeks of classes that next fall. While in Alaska, I had some fraternity brothers covering my classes to provide notes. Complicating matters, I continued partying and bartending when I returned to Akron.

By the end of the Winter Quarter in early 1970, I had a 1.92 grade point average. Clearly nothing to be proud about. I had not dedicated myself to studying, instead I pursued a major in partying. It also meant I lost my draft deferment, which was the concern of every young man in America at the time. I totally fucked up this easy assignment. My immature actions were a big disappointment to my parents.

I received not only a notice from the school of my academic probation, but a letter from the SSS notifying me that I lost my deferment and I was drafted into the U.S. Army. I was sent a round-trip ticket for a bus ride to the Cleveland Armed Forces Induction

Center to take the Army physical. If I passed, I would be inducted into the U.S. Army. That letter from the SSS was not surprising and probably should have been expected.

I did not share that information with anyone at the frat house — that was not something I wanted to advertise as the former Scholarship Chairman. I certainly never told my parents since I did not want them to know of my failure. I was not sure when I would tell them.

Secret Pledge

My brother had just returned from Viet Nam alive with no physical injury. I was not sure how he felt after spending a year in combat after losing several friends who were killed in Viet Nam. There was no point in telling him that I was drafted and adding more to his plate now that he had returned and was trying to acclimate to civilian life, a hard task for many Viet Nam Veterans. I did not want to add my own problems onto what he was dealing with.

I had to accept the reality that I would be in the U.S. Army and probably going to combat. I accepted that fate. My dad always told me, "Your actions have consequences." This induction letter was the consequence of my actions.

I reported to the bus station on a bright and sunny but cold winter morning in Akron, Ohio. I had a hangover headache from partying the night before to go along with my bad attitude of having to begin living the penance for my failures.

At the bus station, I was toward the end of the line and saw the backs of the guys ahead of me. I began sizing them up as I did when competing against my opponents. I wondered how many of these guys could pass the U.S. Army physical. At the time, about 75 percent of draft eligible men were able to pass the physical.

Amazingly, today about 75 percent of the men taking military physicals fail to pass. Ironically in 2025, Robert F Kennedy, Jr. is advancing a program to make our youth healthy again. That is admirable. Indirectly, he will be building back our country's warrior youth.

I should have considered the guys on the bus as my future teammates rather than competition but that was not my mindset that morning. Despite my drinking and partying, I never missed a workout and at 6 foot, 195 pounds and being a college-level athlete, I knew I would pass the physical. I was sure I would do well in basic training.

After receiving the induction letter from the SSS, I started tapering off on my drinking and increasing my workouts to get ready for basic training. The night before was an exception. Maybe I needed liquid courage to forget what a failure I had become.

Gary Ward, a fraternity brother, and I had previously joined a karate dojo in Akron. I was spending time practicing karate instead of staying devoted to my studies. The karate class was a course I never missed. That was the only class I excelled in that year. Unfortunately, that did not help my grade point average. I now considered my additional fighting skill set might come in handy at boot camp or in combat, if needed.

I not only had a bad hangover but a bad attitude. In looking back, perhaps I developed that after coming back from Alaska trying to adjust to college life. I wondered how soldiers adjusted to civilian life when deployed far longer than I was in Alaska and in a more dangerous environment.

As I got on the transport bus to Cleveland, I wondered how the others on the bus got there. I asked myself whether they were just not smart enough to maintain their draft deferment? I clearly had a bad attitude and looked down on the guys on the bus for that. I found a window seat toward the back of the bus.

I squinted to see out the window, which made my hangover worse. It was then I caught a reflection of myself in the bus window, and in that moment I realized that I was one of those guys who was not smart enough to maintain their deferment. I simply did not use my abilities to succeed. I wasted my gifts as a good student and athlete. I had lost my way. As I looked at my reflection in the window, I realized that I had made a major mistake again in failing to apply myself to my studies, compounding the mistake I made by giving up my full-ride football scholarship. I hated that person that I saw staring back at me.

I managed to flunk out of school, I had already walked away from my football scholarship even though the coaches at Akron were great and gave me every opportunity to succeed. I did well on the team, lettering on the JV team and calling defensive signals as well as dressing as a freshman for all the varsity home games. I managed to fuck up that great opportunity. I also lost the opportunity to be an officer in the Air Force.

I also thought about all of the girls I had spent time with. Starting school at Akron, I had a steady high school girlfriend. She was a beautiful young lady who was a dead ringer for a young Goldie Hawn. I continued dating her while I was at Akron, but I also started dating some college girls. I was responsible for ruining the relationship with my high school girlfriend at some point during my first year in college. I dated some beautiful college women at Akron and had some great times. I even scored a date with Miss Ohio, one additional item to add to my dating bucket list.

Fighting Regrets

I also thought about how I ruined too many great relationships with some outstanding women. I chased away everyone who loved me. I was not a good boyfriend. I was the guy in the Eric Church song, "Hell of a View," or Dirks Bentley's song "What Was I Thinkin?" where the parents disapproved of their daughters' choice of a boyfriend.

I was actually confronted by a father of one of the girls I was dating when I stopped to pick her up. He quickly determined that I was not the guy he wanted his daughter to be dating. He had a rifle sitting next to him and as I recall, he was wearing a white tank top/wife beater shirt. Whether the rifle was loaded or not, I got the message and left promptly.

I never picked fights growing up. As a young man my dad taught me to box and defend myself well. He warned me never to pick a fight or be a bully. He did tell me however that if I had to be in a fight, to finish it off with devastating force just as he had instructed the troops under his command at the Battle of the Bulge. Especially when it came to bullies. I did seem to have a lot of confrontations and fights with guys over the girls I dated.

I still have a large scar on my left forearm and upper elbow from getting my first beat down on the Fourth of July in 1965 over my Goldie Hawn-lookalike girlfriend. I was confronted at a fireworks show at the large field behind George Daniel football stadium in Lorain. It was at this same stadium a little less than five years prior that John F. Kennedy gave his presidential campaign speech for the 1960 election.

The day before this incident, I had injured my arm on a construction site, tearing open my left forearm up to the bend in my elbow, requiring 60 stitches and requiring me to have my arm wrapped and in a sling with my arm being immobile. Not a good condition to be in to defend yourself in a fight. I was with a good childhood friend that night, Tony Costello and two other friends.

I first noted a pack of guys headed toward me. They confronted me since one of them considered my girlfriend to be his girl. Immediately I recognized we would be in a fight with a much older and bigger bunch of guys. My other two friends peeled off and probably rightly so under the circumstances. I did not blame them. We were younger and outnumbered. Tony bravely stepped up knowing we were outnumbered with a half dozen older and larger guys with bad intentions heading toward me. Tony took on the leader of the group. A noble gesture, but being younger and smaller, Tony lost the fight. The bullies were emboldened.

Sun Tzu, in *The Art of War* states: "The wise warrior avoids the battle." And further, "If your enemy is in superior strength, evade him."

Great advice, but I was surrounded before I had a chance to avoid this fight. I was also handicapped with my left arm already damaged and in a sling. My enemy clearly had superior strength. No evasion tactics could be deployed, with the only avenue being avoidance of the battle. I tried to use my negotiating skills since I could not defend myself with one arm in a sling.

As I was attempting to advocate a truce, I was sucker punched to the left side of my face. My left arm could not have blocked the punch even had I seen it coming. I then had to block off shots flying in from all angles.They kicked my ass pretty good. This was the first of many run-ins with boyfriends or ex-boyfriends.

After the fight, Tony and I had to limp back to our homes on West 40th Street, about a mile and a half away. We were not talking. The only positive thought I could take away from this beat down was having a friend like Tony Costello stand up for me against some tough odds. Tony died a few years back in a terrible truck accident. I wrote a eulogy for Tony to make sure his family knew what a heroic son they had. How many friends would sacrifice themselves like he did for me?

As we walked home that night, I held my left arm with my right hand to stop the bleeding. I noticed my vision in my left eye was getting shrouded since the left side of my face was swelling up from the beating. It hurt to breathe due to the kicks to my ribs. It was at that moment I felt something: It was that big chip on my shoulder, born on the Fourth of July. I vowed that this was never going to happen again. I would never let a bully intimidate or defeat me. I have kept that chip on my shoulder and it has served me well, especially when confronted by a bullying attorney who may try to intimidate my client or me.

I managed to make it home. My parents were on our back porch enjoying a holiday drink poolside that hot July evening. I was too embarrassed to let them see me, so I just yelled out through the back screen door that I was going to bed. I recall wrapping my arm tightly in a kitchen towel and crawling into bed.

At the breakfast table the next morning, I could no longer hide my beat down. My left eye was swollen shut with other visible bruises on my face.

My brother was at the breakfast table and asked me who beat my ass and why. I headed back to the emergency room to have my arm stitched up. I learned what a Z-plasty is. I still have a large "Z" scar on my left arm and each time I look at it I remind myself that I will always be prepared.

Ken and his best friend, Bob Nagy, tracked down two of those guys. They beat the living shit out of them, although they could not track down the ringleader and boyfriend. That was payback for what they did. It's what I believe all young men back in the day did in those circumstances to protect the family honor. It was also good training for their future combat careers in Viet Nam. I would have to wait years before I found the bully that started the fight.

A few years later I took the same Goldie Hawn-lookalike girlfriend on a date. We left the theatre that snowy night and headed to my Imperial to warm up. While walking by a pool hall adjacent to the Amherst theatre, three guys with pool sticks in their hands were in the doorway, saw my gorgeous girlfriend and started taunting me with some verbal shots.

I did not like the odds. As my dad had taught me, I walked past them to avoid the fight. I thought we escaped that confrontation, however after the third nasty taunt my girlfriend stopped and gave me that look that every young man knows: without saying anything her facial expression told me that if I did not respond to those taunts I was not much of a man. No choice now. I stopped walking.

As I turned to confront the three thugs, two things quickly ran through my mind. The first thought was that the last time I was in Amherst was for an evening football scrimmage in the summer when some hotshot on the Amherst Comets football team caught me with a wicked forearm under my face mask splattering my nose. As I braced to confront my three potential attackers, I told myself that shit was not happening tonight. These guys were not breaking my nose and they were not going to get a headshot on me. I prepared to fight and defend.

The second thought was a flashback to my Fourth of July beat down as I now confronted three potential attackers, odds against me again. Lucky for me I also saw over the shoulder of the bully of the group, some of my teammates on the football team heading our way as they exited the theatre. I felt better since I now had back up so that the two assholes with the Alpha dog would not be breaking a pool stick over my head while I fought.

I squared up with the leader of this trio and got into my right-handed fighting stance. My dad taught me to fight right-handed even though I was left hand predominant. I shot a rifle and pistol and wrote left-handed. In fact, I shot pool left handed. My dad thought my left-hand dominant would make my left jab snap and my left hook all that more potent. He was right. I had on my winter leather gloves, so I had some padding which made striking my opponent's head much like hitting a heavy bag as I was used to doing.

My opponent however was tougher than I thought. I had landed several left-right combinations to his head and recall that he could take a good punch. However, I was a superior boxer to this guy. I blocked his big right-hand haymaker and after a few more combinations I dropped him onto the icy sidewalk with a powerful right cross. Amazingly, he still would not give up so I had to continue to beat on him while on the sidewalk. He would not tap out. I had no other choice so I had to close this fight out by grabbing his head and began bashing it into the icy parking meter pole on the sidewalk to finish off this fight. This did not stop until some older men pulled me off him. The optics looked as though I was trying to kill him, which may have been the case had I not been dragged off him. In hindsight I was glad these men pulled me off him.

This fight over the same girl went a lot better than the first fight over her. I found out the next day that the guy I fought was one of if not the toughest guys in Amherst. Splash one tough bully. I am not sure that is what all young men my age in America did in these circumstances, but that is what the guys I knew did and was part of how we were raised. My confrontations with guys over girls did not stop there.

A few guys on the Akron football team and I made a big mistake by going into the Diamond Grill in downtown Akron. The Diamond Grill was an historic bar and restaurant just off campus, generally frequented by townies and not Akron students. We walked in with our letter jackets on and began flirting with what we thought were some available girls. Big mistake since we obviously were intruding into the love life of a couple of these townies. We quickly got the message and left, but we were jumped in the parking lot. I did okay with my opponent, essentially coming to a draw, but several of my buddies got their asses beat pretty good. Another fight caused by chasing girls. It would not end there.

I had the same issues involving girls and fights with guys when I bartended at the Draught House on Turkey Foot Road just outside of Akron. You were the "man" as a bartender if you had the strength and balance to carry six full pitchers of beer, three in each hand and not spill the beer as you served your customers. It was especially important that you did not spill it on your Draught House vest, which had its own consequences.

One night a group of rowdy Kent State athletes in their letter jackets were circling a table of young ladies, one of which I was flirting with. I was dropping off a pitcher at her table and exchanging some pick up lines when one of the Kent hot shots bumped into me while I was balancing six pitchers of beer, causing me to spill some of the beer all over my Draught House vest.

When I confronted these guys standing there with beer dripping down my Draught House vest, they pushed me, told me to fuck off and be on my way. Another group of bullies. Not much I could do at that moment since I was carrying six pitchers of beer. Spilling beer onto my vest was a big no-no since that meant I had to buy a round at the end of the night for my fellow bartenders, two of which were my fraternity brothers, Ken Shoemaker and Tom "Goose" Gooseman. I knew I was going to have to pay up. On top of that, as a bartender at the Draught House, we were instructed not to take shit from the patrons.

Immediately after serving my pitchers to several other tables I came back and confronted these guys. I squared off with the arrogant bully who I found out later was on the Kent wrestling team. My fight strategy after looking at him was that I was not going to wrestle this guy and needed to take him out from a distance. I squared up in my fighting stance and hit him with a straight right hand to the jaw, knocking him out with my first punch. I thought "Down goes Letterman!"

He was knocked out cold and did not get up. I also thought Marine Lance Corporal Ray Hodorowski would have been proud of me as he looked down on me from heaven and admired the fighting skills I developed since I boxed with him. I hoped Ray would be proud of that knockout punch I delivered, just like the one he delivered to me. But this fight was not over.

We were closing out the registers at the end of the night when one of the other bartenders walked in the back room and indicated that a half dozen guys from Kent waited in the back parking lot for me. There was no place to hide since the club had closed and most of the patrons had gone home. I looked out and it was the Kent Lettermen in full force. I counted six or more and quickly accepted the wise warrior's concept of avoiding battle, especially when the enemy was of superior strength. I had to figure out how we would evade the superior force.

I did have an out as each night we could count on some bartender groupies to hang out at last call and see if they could hook up with us. My buddy Goose was already speaking to two of them. We asked these ladies if we could spend the night with them and could they pick us up at the side entrance to the club. They did and we headed to their place leaving our car encircled by the Kent Lettermen.

Evasion complete, though that turned into a late night off campus with these young ladies. And, of course, that again meant no morning classes. You can see a pattern emerging and why I was not attending class and my grades were suffering. That lifestyle led me to being on that bus ride.

I am not sure why I was thinking of all this on the way to the Induction Center, maybe I was trying to make sense of what led me to this moment. I suppose blaming it on chasing girls was easier than admitting that I was a failure by choice.

All of these thoughts rolled through my head on that hour-long bus ride. Perhaps I realized that all that fun was ending and I would be paying the piper. I felt like the guy who got caught committing a crime trying to justify why he was on the transport bus headed to prison, but in my case, figuratively a bus ride to Viet Nam. Those negative thoughts didn't help my hangover, so I decided to take a nap.

CHAPTER 22

Induction Into The Army

TAKING THE OATH AND A CHANGE OF ATTITUDE

I awoke from my nap when our transport bus hit a bump. I opened my eyes and we approached downtown Cleveland.

I always had fond memories of going to Cleveland. I recalled some great Indians baseball games and Browns football games, which included my dad taking me to the 1964 NFL Championship when I was 13 years old. The Browns beat the Baltimore Colts 27-0, their last NFL Championship.

Our high school football team also took many bus rides to the Cleveland area. A small Catholic High School, we never played the big Catholic high schools in Cleveland - St. Ed's or St. Ignatius - just because of the size difference. We had about only 140 boys in our four grades to their approximate 1,000. We did get to play the smaller Catholic schools in the Cleveland area, like Parma Byzantine and Cleveland Central Catholic. These Cleveland Catholic schools, even though smaller than the large schools, always had more students than Lorain St. Mary's.

However, we never lost to a Cleveland high school in my junior or senior year. Taking those road trips and defeating our opponents were always fond memories.

As I looked out the window and saw Cleveland's street scenes, I recalled one afternoon in my senior year in high school. Mike Coughlin, our Class A all-state running back and I decided to take off for part of the day to go to the Roxy Burlesque, an old-fashioned strip club in downtown Cleveland. Our plan was that we'd sneak out of school, drive to the club and get in with our fake IDs. Our buddies would cover for us and we would be back in time for football practice. That plan was working well.

We got into the club and were entertained by the strippers. When we got back, however, head football coach Tim Rose called us into his office. We knew we were caught and thought he would give us hell for leaving school without permission. Coach Rose was a strict disciplinarian but that afternoon he seemed oddly calm but disappointed. We explained what happened and Coach Rose calmly told us exactly what my dad had taught me: *"Your actions have consequences."*

Coach Rose was a taskmaster, so it was unusual for him to be so calm. I soon understood why he acted so professionally and somewhat sympathetic to us when he told us an assistant football coach and a recruiter from Colgate University both came specifically to our school to see me and Mike.

I knew Mike already had a number of full rides to Big Ten schools and would pass on an offer from Colgate. Not so with me. I received offers but not from top Division I schools. However, I did have the grades and skill set to compete well in the Ivy League. I would have loved the chance to play for Colgate.

My parents would have been proud of me for getting a scholarship and graduating with an Ivy League degree. When I heard that a coach from Colgate and his recruiter were at the school when we were gone I realized that great opportunity was gone forever. Actions certainly do have consequences.

From the perspective of the Colgate assistant and his recruiter, being told that a potential recruit left school to go to a strip club during the school day did not reflect well on me as Ivy League material. I could tell from the look on Coach Rose's face that he wanted to punish us but realized we had already punished ourselves.

I never heard back from the Colgate coach, and rightfully so. Partying at a strip club meant I was on to the University of Akron on a full football scholarship. However, it was a great afternoon at the strip club and another fond memory of Cleveland; but chasing after women continued to cause problems for me.

Back To Reality

By this point my headache had gone away and I found myself with a smile on my face as I thought of my great times in Cleveland. I wasn't sure where getting inducted into the U.S. Army would rank in those Cleveland memories and adventures.

The bus pulled to a stop and we departed to enter the facility. I paid attention to what took place and stopped thinking about old memories. I would soon become a man entering the army. Time to put away childish things and focus on reality.

I shuffled off the bus with the other draft candidates. I spoke with one of the recruiting sergeants. He struck me as a dedicated soldier. He looked and acted the part.

I took my physical. I passed the U.S. Army physical with flying colors. I tried to focus on the positive since being shipped off to Viet Nam would probably be my next challenge. I would need to train and be ready to fight.

I thought about losing my draft deferment, being inducted into the U.S. Army and heading to Viet Nam as penance for my immature acts. It was either going to be penance or hell. I would soon find out in the coming months. I actually looked forward to it and the challenge of the army obstacle course that I heard so much about.

My opportunity to be the first person in my family to go to college ended. I did not know how I would explain this to my parents. I would have to tell them at some point. I was certain they would be disappointed and unhappy over my failed college performance. I put that thought in the back of my head and paid attention.

We proceeded to another room at the induction center. I looked on the bright side: I'd end up in boot camp. I looked forward to it, much like I was used to doing every summer in two-a-days for football. Perhaps that discipline is what I needed. Standing in the line getting processed was my new reality.

I recall that something happened that day, which I did not expect. Our group was addressed as potential members of the U.S. Army. The officer in charge advised of the honor we would have in taking the oath to become members of the United States Armed Forces. I raised my right hand, took the oath and was sworn in:

"I, do solemnly swear that I will support and defend the Constitution of the United States against all enemies, foreign and domestic; that I will bear true faith and allegiance to the same; and that I will obey the orders of the President of the United States and the orders of the officers appointed over me. So help me God."

As I took the oath, I felt something. I now joined the ranks of the other dedicated American soldiers who came before me like my brother, my dad and all of the local neighborhood friends who served, some who never returned.

Perhaps I would make a difference? I knew it would be tough but I was up for the challenge. I knew that I would have to change my lifestyle. I committed to do that.

We got to meet some of the officers there and spoke with the recruiting sergeant before we left. I was impressed. At the end of the day, we got on the bus and returned home.

My thoughts on the bus ride back differed greatly than on the way to the induction center. I thought about the oath I had just taken. I would have no problem with taking orders from commanding officers or sergeants like I met today who I respected. They were men proven in battle and in my eyes, warriors. I questioned whether I would ever have followed a direct order from the prior Commander in Chief, President Johnson.

I despised President Johnson for the way he prosecuted the war as well as the questions surrounding Kennedy being assassinated in Johnson's home state of Texas. I also questioned Johnson's actions in addressing Viet Nam by initiating and pursuing a seemingly never-ending war which seemed to have no real purpose and was orchestrated, in my opinion, by petty politicians like himself. Those thoughts fueled my disgust with the former Commander in Chief. These politicians used my friends as cannon fodder. To me, the Viet Nam War was not being fought wisely. As it progressed and ramped up it had begun snatching the lives of our friends as well as scarring those who returned.

I recalled the Sun Tzu maxim that fit Johnson as well as the military industrial complex at the time, which said: "It is only one who is thoroughly acquainted with the evils of war that can thoroughly understand the profitable way of carrying it on."

Sun Tzu did not know it but he was describing Johnson, a power hungry, corrupt politician that destroyed people's lives for his benefit and that of his cronies. Johnson is credited with passing the Civil Rights Bill of 1964, a bill similar to the Civil Rights Bill of 1957 that Johnson himself intentionally blocked when he was in the Senate and President Eisenhower wanted to pass a bill for civil rights reform.

Johnson did not want the Republicans to get credit for the bill. So, Johnson blocked implementation of the bill with his racist allies in Congress and did so for more than seven years, depriving the country and specifically African Americans of that much needed law. Johnson, with much bravado, then stepped up and proclaimed that he was the *new white civil rights leader.* This hypocritical politician signed into law the Civil Rights Bill of 1964 and bragged about the control he would have over African Americans with some reports indicating he said: "I'll have those ni - - - rs voting Democratic for 200 years."

Johnson was a reprehensible human being who sought and wielded power for his own purposes and that of his friends. He had just left office before I was inducted into the Army but his fingerprints were all over the war plans as well as on the graves of our friends.

I always felt that Johnson was the "Usurper to the Throne" and I believe that he was the evil Claudius in this modern tragedy that played out on the American stage.

As I sat on that bus on the way back to Akron, I did not know that had Kennedy not been killed, the Viet Nam War would not have been conducted in the manner Johnson handled it. I only knew that Johnson was a prick for killing off my friends in a seemingly endless war with no purpose other than the death and injury to young men my age all across America.

I also did not know the quote at the time, but Sun Tzu had already stated what I felt: "There is no instance of a nation benefitting from prolonged warfare."

I promised myself that I would honor the oath I had just taken and follow orders from my commanding officers notwithstanding my feelings about Johnson. I respected all of the brave men and women who followed orders. I would follow that tradition.

I also considered that I was now inducted and an official member of the *Warrior Class* that every great country needs from its young men. It was a commitment.

This for me was an opportunity to correct my downward trajectory. I realized my lifestyle of dating, partying and drinking would not serve me well. I regretted my immaturity and hoped for another chance at college and a career.

That dream was now four years away. Assuming I fought well and returned from Viet Nam alive, I'd dedicate myself to fighting hard, surviving and getting a college degree.

Getting ready for basic training was my new focus. I thought if I had to go to that jungle hell hole, I would like to give orders rather than be a grunt taking orders. I thought about committing to becoming either a noncommissioned officer running a platoon or ultimately getting into officer's candidate school so I could run my own company like my dad.

That was my initial thought when I enrolled into the ROTC program at Akron, but that goal was no longer available to me. I now had new goals.

I felt better on the way back to Akron then on the way to Cleveland. Perhaps the hangover was wearing off slightly or seeing some of the dedicated officers and sergeants running the induction center and taking the oath of office to become a soldier changed my mood. I could despise the politicians for getting us into the war, but the men I met at the induction center had my respect.

They were dedicated American Soldiers. They swore to fight, even if they did not agree with the policies. I would fight by their side. My respect for them was immediate and my new focus shifted to getting ready for basic training.

I heard a few guys talking on the bus, concerned about the physical and mental stress of basic training. I was pretty sure a lot of them would struggle to survive college football two-a-days or the Oklahoma drill where 195-pound linebackers like me faced significantly heavier offensive tackles. I also had a taste of mental challenges not only from summer football, but also from *Hell Week* that I went through for the fraternity.

Amazingly, I saw the vast majority of my pledge class members, many of whom were on the football team with me or were on the basketball or wrestling team, all break down because of the mental fatigue of having no sleep and having constant harassment around the clock. As the "Jap" of the pledge class, I had to take more than anyone else. I never broke.

I thought basic training would be challenging, but quite frankly, I looked forward to it. I really didn't have anything else to look forward to. Akron kicked me out of school and I lost my full ride in football.

My life had consisted of partying and ruining one relationship after another by chasing off every girl that loved me. Not much to put on your resume. I began to realize that my new path was the consequences of my own actions. Service in the U.S. Army was the new reality that I accepted.

I recall returning to the fraternity house, grabbing a beer, eating something and laying down. I did not tell anyone what took place that day. I had not told anyone about my induction letter.

How do you admit to being the ultimate loser that forfeited a football scholarship, flunked out of school, was drafted and then inducted into the U.S. Army? Nah, I was not sharing that sad song story with anyone at the frat house.

I went to my room and dozed off.

CHAPTER 23

A Mother's Love

CHALLENGING THE DRAFT
ON BEHALF OF HER YOUNGEST SON

For the second day in a row, one of my fraternity brothers woke me at the fraternity house.

I was pissed off because I did not plan on waking up that early — no classes other than my late afternoon karate class. I was told that my parents were on the fraternity house phone and wondered where I had been the day before.

Apparently, they called the frat house on several occasions the day before when I got inducted into the U.S. Army in Cleveland. No one could tell them where I was, I never got the message and didn't tell anyone what I did. My parents were concerned.

I returned their call. That was not pleasant. I confessed what happened, admitted to my failures and informed them that not only was I on academic probation, but that I had been inducted into the U.S. Army the day before.

I explained what took place and advised them that I would leave for basic training in the coming weeks. I used the two years of Latin studies in Catholic school and told them, "*Alea iacta est*," which means the die was cast. Perhaps a little dramatic but this was a major life change.

My parents did not appreciate the high-brow reference to Latin studies when I had just lost my deferment due to my academic probation. They clearly did not like my casual attitude in accepting what was sure to be a tour in Viet Nam. They were rightfully upset.

I was a major disappointment to them. I wasted my talent and ability. They were not happy that I did not tell them I had already been inducted. They asked me the rhetorical question: *With your intelligence, how is it possible for you not to maintain a C average at Akron?*

After hearing that question, I recognized how pathetic my academic efforts were. I also recognized that I had given them more worries at a time when they were literally losing their home and their business. They did not deserve this from their youngest son. I had lost my way.

My mother was especially upset. To understand her, you need to know that she was a strong-willed, full-blooded Ukrainian.

Mom was one of 10 children growing up in the Carson family. Her mother and father emigrated from Ukraine and settled in South Lorain, close to the U.S. Steel factory. She suffered the loss of a younger brother in a childhood accident on a construction site when he was buried alive. One of her other three brothers was developmentally delayed due to exposure to high levels of alcohol in utero because my grandmother Carson (affectionately called "Baba") drank heavily while she was pregnant with Uncle Johnny.

He actually was a great guy. He worked his entire life as a sanitation worker for the city. Whenever I visited, he and I would always have a few beers together. The dark but good-natured joke we had with Uncle Johnny was that he started drinking at an early age - before he was born.

My mom's father Walter (Valter in Ukrainian) was a heavy alcoholic. He died before I was old enough to meet him. My mom quit school in 11th grade to support her family. I was proud of Mom, since even though she had to sacrifice her opportunity to finish high school, she did not give up on her education. She spoke three languages fluently (Ukrainian, Polish and English with a little Russian).

One of her brothers, my Uncle Myron, in a drunken rage, shot his wife, my aunt and then tried to commit suicide. You had to be tough to grow up in that household.

I enjoyed Baba Carson but her demeanor was totally different from my other grandmother, Stephanie Jurczynski, who never drank or had a harsh word.

I also did not find it odd that at the Russian Orthodox celebration of Christmas (Orthodox churches in Russia, Serbia and Ukraine celebrate Christmas on Jan. 6) when all the young men in the Carson family that turned 12 years old (or perhaps younger) were drinking shots of whiskey or vodka at Baba's house with our uncles. This is what Ukrainians do, at least that was my Russian Orthodox Christmas experience at my grandmother's house. That is the household in which my mom was raised.

Years later I introduced my beautiful fiancé Darlene Deem to my Ukrainian grandmother at that same house in South Lorain. Baba had Darlene sit down in the dining room and started questioning her. Baba then got right to the point as she challenged Darlene to shoot shots of whiskey as she poured one after the other into shot glasses, which she had lined up on her huge dining room table (it had to seat a family of 12 at one time).

Baba was barely 5-foot and about a 100 pounds soaking wet, but boy could she drink. She would ask Darlene a question and then after each answer she'd shout, "*You* d*rr*ink," in her heavy Ukrainian accent.

I was proud of Darlene who slammed back three shots in a row like a trooper. Baba would ask her a question and after Darlene answered, she was ordered to slam back a full shot of whiskey. Darlene gained the seal of approval from my grandmother as being acceptable as my future wife to enter the family and for being able to withstand that Ukrainian interview.

Baba labeled her a "*hilly-billy*" because Darlene was from West Virginia. So, from context, that is the household my mom grew up in. My mom was not shy about stating her position since you had to be strong growing up in that environment.

My mom married my father at the U.S. Army Air base in Wichita, Kansas only to see him leave right after their honeymoon for World War II. She prayed he would return alive.

At the time I had confessed to her about my induction into the U.S. Army, Mom had spent the past several years worrying about her other son Ken coming home alive since he had already been in combat in Viet Nam. My mom also had to console several other mothers in our neighborhood whose sons had already been killed in Viet Nam. She had attended a number of funerals for the neighborhood friends that came home from Viet Nam in body bags.

Mom also lost my oldest brother in childbirth. She was steeled in the knowledge of death and worry over the soldiers in her family coming home from war. She apparently made up her mind she was not going to worry about her youngest son becoming the third member of her immediate family she had to hope would come home alive from a war. She vowed not to lose another son.

My mom raised holy hell with me on the phone. She did not stop there. She made it her mission to notify our local congressman that she would not accept that her only two living sons both had to serve in combat in Viet Nam.

Mom was not at all happy when my brother Ken actively solicited a combat assignment in Viet Nam rather than remain and serve his time in a cushy job in Germany.

His decision to volunteer for combat was at a time when our childhood friends returned to Lorain dead. She decided that she would not go through that agony again.

Speaking with our local Congressman, Mom obtained legal counsel and pursued a petition under the Sullivan Act that I would not have to deploy to Viet Nam or even serve in the U.S. Army. I was not involved in any of these efforts and knew nothing about this. While this went on I was at the fraternity house in Akron, preparing to report to basic training. Looking back, I feel sorry for the U.S. Army officer on the receiving end of my mom's effort. She was anything if not a persistent and determined Ukrainian that would not accept no for an answer.

Mom notified me that I would not report to basic training nor would I be in the U.S. Army. However, I also no longer would be at Akron. She said I had to leave the fraternity house, come home and work to earn money for tuition and board the next year.

I also had to enroll at another university to change my environment. The plea bargain apparently made for me was that I had to commit to keeping up my grades, study criminal justice, get into law enforcement or some form of law, and attend school with my brother. Ken already made a decision that he would start at Kent State University in its criminal justice program the following year.

My life plans changed again. I also would go to Kent State, provided I could get in with the scholastic record I had posted at Akron.

Mom said that I had to commit to being a serious student and follow the directions imposed upon me. She added that if my grades fell off below acceptable levels, I would lose my second deferment, and my ass would absolutely be shipped out to Viet Nam. So, I was given a second chance that I never thought would be possible.

My parents told me the news about the change in plans and thought that I would be relieved.

Quite frankly, at the time I didn't give a shit one way or the other and told them that. I still had a poor attitude about school and I looked forward to basic training. I was prepared to accept the consequences of my actions, serving in the U.S. Army and perhaps a combat tour in Viet Nam. That fate I had accepted.

Mom said to change my attitude, go to Kent State and commit to being a serious student. Again, there was no debating her when she made a point.

However, I still had to get admitted. Fortunately for me, my prior high undergraduate grades, college admission scores and the fact I was at one time on the dean's list at Akron got me into Kent. I explained that I had turned over a new leaf and was committed to studying. Otherwise, I would head to Viet Nam. And break my mom's heart.

I left Akron, a conservative, blue-collar industrial-based town –

just like where I grew up. I also left all my friends in the fraternity and my teammates on the University of Akron football team. I enjoyed being with all those guys, perhaps too much. Many of the guys I played with on the University of Akron football team came from Catholic high schools like I went to. Some of the guys went to Saint V's and Archbishop Hoban in Akron. All of us played in our own version of the football "Holy Wars" in high school where the top Catholic schools in the area fought each other for the conference or area championships, as I did with Lorain St. Mary vs. our arch rival, Elyria Catholic. I would miss leaving my teammates at Akron and my fraternity brothers, a regret I still carry with me, but I had no one to blame but myself.

For all the partying we did, the Lambda Chi Alpha fraternity did have a noble purpose and was founded on Christian principles. Our motto was *Vir Quisqe Vir*, a phrase taken from the Bible meaning *"Every Man a Man."* This motto is considered a cornerstone of the Lambda Chi Alpha philosophy, emphasizing personal responsibility and accountability.

Probably a lifestyle I should have adopted. Had I followed the fraternity pledge, I would not have been facing some of the obstacles before me. The concept of *Vir Quisque Vir* was that every one of us on Earth is created equal and should be treated with respect. I left that brotherhood behind.

I went to Kent State, a liberal arts college that, while only 15 miles away from Akron, might as well have been on another planet. I went from blue-collar conservatism to a large state university that was the epicenter of the anti-war protest in America.

I would study for a criminal justice degree where four students had been murdered by Ohio National Guard members for exercising their right to free speech. Quite a dynamic shift in college surroundings. Fraternity and football life vs. anti-war protests. Mentally, I shifted gears, and fast. From nearly being shipped off to war and being proud to serve to rubbing shoulders with banner-carrying, long-haired protestors shouting about the evils of the Viet Nam War.

It was going to be quite a change. I focused on finishing college in this environment. But it didn't matter what I thought. I had no choice. This was my last chance to become the first member of my family to graduate from college.

My plan at Kent State was to enroll in a pre-law program and get into Criminal Justice Studies. My application occurred in the Spring of 1970, at the time there was the national incident on the Kent State campus where the four students were killed and nine others wounded during a Viet Nam War protest.

Perhaps the Kent admissions officer, knowing that I was drafted and inducted into the U.S. Army but now applying to Kent State, thought for some reason I was some type of refugee from the Viet Nam draft or a war protestor. I said I was inducted into the U.S. Army but did not serve. This was an odd situation. I was definitely not a conscientious objector, a war protestor, and certainly not a draft dodger.

I was granted admission into Kent and entered its Criminal Justice program, recognized as the best program in Ohio. I wondered if one of the classes would cover the criminality of our politicians as to how they prosecuted the Viet Nam War, tacitly killing off my childhood friends? Or perhaps a chapter or two on how the government authorized armed soldiers to open fire on peaceful protestors on a college campus, killing four of them?

My brother had thankfully returned from Viet Nam alive. He and I reunited at Kent when he was admitted the following year so we would finish our college education together, both getting degrees in Criminal Justice and getting exposed to an extraordinary college life during a turbulent time in U.S. history. That experience was priceless.

I have always thought that my brother's courage in volunteering for combat to take someone else's place was a major factor in the U.S. Army's decision to reinstate my deferment. That, along with my mother's persistent petitioning of the army, allowed me to avoid military service and a trip to Viet Nam.

The army perhaps noted my father's heroic service record as a U.S. Army captain who fought in the Battle of the Bulge. Or maybe they simply wanted to silence a strong vocal Ukrainian lady who was single-minded in her goal not to agonize over another loved one sent off to war.

I did not have the answer, but I was given that one last chance to turn my life around.

While I will always be grateful for what my brother and my parents did for me, one thought always crossed my mind: If I was relieved of going to serve, what other American mother had to worry about her own son taking my place as draftee JFK #160 in Viet Nam? Whatever happened to that young man that took my place? The survivor's guilt of not serving in Viet Nam has always been in the back of my mind. I always wondered what military life was like for the guy that took my spot. Was he able to handle the pressure of combat? Did he suffer any ill effects from serving in my spot? Was he brave in combat? Did he return home safe?

That survivor's guilt remains with me. I had no joy in avoiding service in the military. Notwithstanding those thoughts, none of the events have reduced my admiration or respect for those brave soldiers who did serve in that bloody war. They were American Soldiers.

CHAPTER 24

Kent State

1970 AND THE CONTINUING WAR PROTESTS

The difference between the University of Akron and Kent State University in the fall of 1970 was stark.

Akron was an in-city university and its campus was situated in the downtown area of a bustling blue-collar community, then the fourth largest city in Ohio. A large percentage of the students commuted from their homes in Akron.

Kent State on the other hand was located in a small town of less than 30,000 people just 15 miles from Akron in a beautiful country setting. Kent's lush country campus was more than three times the size of Akron's urban campus with a high percentage of the students from other states.

Akron was a townie-populated university of commuters with a modest on-campus student body, whereas Kent was a destination university. Kent also had a great reputation as a college for educators in addition to having a well-respected criminal justice program.

So, I went from conservative, urban commuter university to a rural liberal arts university which became the epicenter of the counterculture in America.

President Richard Nixon made an effort to end the long drawn-out Viet Nam War started by his predecessor, Lyndon Johnson —

a political gangster. Nixon tried to negotiate an honorable peace from a position of strength by selectively bombing North Viet Nam and also bombing the routes used by North Viet Nam and the Viet Cong through Cambodia while authorizing attacks on Cambodia.

That was viewed by many as an escalation of the war and an invasion of another country, triggering mass protests on many college campuses against the war. At Kent State, a peaceful protest on May 4, 1970 ended with the Ohio National Guard opening fire on students, killing four of the 13 people that were shot. The nine others suffered gunshot wounds, some of whom were not even a part of the protest.

The shootings at Kent State marked the first time our military opened fire on civilians on a college campus in response to an anti-war protest. The only comparable event was the year before, when the South Carolina Highway Patrol opened fire on a group of protesting students at South Carolina State College based upon protests over segregation.

Before the shootings, tension on campuses throughout America intensified. These frustrations boiled over tragically at Kent State. The school closed days after the shootings and did not reopen until the fall of 1970. That was my first day of school.

The Kent State shooting was a major turning point in American history and helped signal the tremendous societal change and resistance to the Viet Nam War. It also helped end the war.

On October 16, 1970 a grand jury convened in Ravenna, Ohio, population just over 10,000 people. Ravenna was the county seat of Portage County. The grand jury was seated to determine the fate of the protestors, 25 of whom were charged with various criminal charges involving the burning of the ROTC building on the Kent campus on May 2. The grand jury also addressed the actions of the Ohio National Guard on May 4, the day the guardsmen opened fire on unarmed protestors on the Commons of Kent State University.

A state court judge from his courtroom in Ravenna would hear the most intensely watched trial in the history of this sleepy town. The overarching legal and societal issues would ask: Was it proper for a military unit of the U.S. Government to open fire on unarmed protestors peacefully exercising their First Amendment rights?

The Posse Comitatus Act of 1878 was passed to prevent the military from enforcing civil law. The act was created to prevent the military from becoming a national police force. Ohio Governor James Rhodes did not care about the Posse Comitatus concept when he unleashed the state's National Guard onto the Kent campus.

This example affected us as a byproduct of the Viet Nam War, where there was no discernible answer. Bill Schroeder was just an innocent student walking to class. While Bill graduated from Lorain High School - a few blocks from where I went to school - I didn't know him, but I would have liked to. The guy was a good athlete, an Eagle Scout. He enrolled in the Reserved Officer Training Corps (ROTC) program. He wasn't even an anti-war protestor. A stray bullet shot by the National Guard on campus breaking up a Viet Nam War protest ended his life that day.

How do you explain the irony of his death as an ROTC student killed by the military he was training to join? How do you brush this off as collateral damage? What would my hometown have been like if Bill and the other 98 young men from Lorain County that died serving in Viet Nam had had a chance to enrich the community? How could you make any sense of what was happening at the time?

Amazingly, the Ohio grand jury deliberating on the Kent State shooting brought no charges against the Ohio National Guard for murder, manslaughter, negligent endangerment or any other charge. Nothing. Not one charge against a government official. Not Gov. Rhodes, who ordered the National Guard onto campus. Not the commanding officers. And not the soldiers. No one was held responsible.

The grand jury however did indict 25 protestors, mostly Kent State students exercising their right to free speech guaranteed by the First Amendment of the United States Constitution, which they exercised by engaging in a protest on May 2 that resulted in the burning of the Reserved Officers Training Building on campus. No one was injured in the incident, but 25 protestors were indicted.

According to an article in *The New York Times* on Dec. 1, 1973, the judge from Ravenna ordered the grand jury results to be burned and not made public. This claim in *The Times* article was questioned with an official response from the Court that there was no formal court ruling made to destroy the grand jury results, the destruction of the evidence just conveniently happened and resulted in all of the grand jury transcripts being destroyed. This never happens with formal court documents but here, when it involved potential misdeeds by the U.S. Government, that just happened, like what happened to the entire Helmich trial file that the Federal Clerk could not locate nor could anyone else.

There was no need for grand jury notes. It was evident in plain sight that the guardsmen marched onto campus and shot 13 unarmed students, but were never charged with one criminal act. Meanwhile 25 protestors were indicted for various felonies.

One of those protestors and the first to be tried for actions to protest the Viet Nam War on campus was Jerry Rupe. Well before his trial, Jerry was one of the first people I met at Kent.

Jerry and I became good friends. I learned quite a bit in my criminal justice studies at Kent State as well as from my conversations with Jerry as to the actions of law enforcement. I learned - both inside and outside of the classroom - as to how the U.S. Government and the judicial system worked. Quite an education.

The criminal jury seated in that case did not convict Jerry on any of the felony charges. He was convicted on a misdemeanor for interfering with a fireman and sentenced to up to six months in jail. No one else was tried, including the government officials or the Ohio National Guard. One protest on May 2. One person was found guilty of a misdemeanor. Yet 13 people were shot on campus. Four killed. Zero indictments. No criminal responsibility for any of the shootings.

Three years later in 1974 there were eight indictments against Ohio National Guardsmen arising out of the Kent shooting. Federal Judge Frank Battisti sitting on the federal bench in Cleveland dismissed all charges directly after the prosecution presented its case, ending any criminal liability by anyone involved in shooting 13 unarmed peaceful U.S. citizen protestors on the Kent campus. As we watched and learned, civil rights in America depended on what right was being asserted and for what cause.

That was justice in America in the 1970s. That fueled my interest in the law, my interest in initially studying criminal justice and then going to law school. It also was a trigger for my interest in representing those who challenged the government's position on the law which resulted in my representation of numerous people and entities challenging state or federal government, including convicted spy Joseph G. Helmich and his claimed manipulation by the CIA to become a minor player in the overall plan to assassinate President John F. Kennedy.

When I first arrived at Kent as it reopened, I needed to find temporary quarters. I knew no one on campus other than a guy from my neighborhood, Mike Ecker. Mike and I played Little League Baseball together when I was an all-star pitcher. I pitched against Mike's team, Ecker Radlow and Desantis and threw a no-hitter, striking out 16 of the 18 batters I faced in the six-inning game. If you can believe it, I struck Mike out three times in that six-inning game. I hoped he did not hold that against me.

Mike was also Jewish as was his roommate so I did not know if that would be an issue with them accepting me as their temporary roommate due to my religion. Most of my friends were Catholic. It worked out great, however. I got along with them and learned a few things about the Jewish culture and shared with them my position on Catholicism, which was founded by Jesus, himself a Jew. We talked about the various rules of each religion and the triggering event, Jesus' trial in front of the Sanhedrin.

We got along well and it gave me a good start at Kent. However, Mike's apartment at the Silver Meadows apartment complex was about four miles from campus. I wanted to be within walking distance of campus but not in a dorm. I was on a limited budget so Mike's apartment was an initial landing ground to get myself acclimated before I could find housing closer to my classes.

I ultimately located a one-bedroom unit on the third floor of an old hotel in downtown Kent, which had just been renovated for student housing and was within a few blocks of campus.

The old Franklin Hotel on Main Street was converted in 1970 to the "Towne House" just before I moved in. This old hotel had a bar on the sixth floor. It had a colorful history, including stays in the hotel by old-time band leaders Glenn Miller and Guy Lombardo. The hotel's history also included an extended stay by Elliot Ness of *"The Untouchables"* fame who was said to regularly frequent the sixth-floor bar. So, not a bad place to study pre-law and criminal justice, living in the same hotel frequented by one of America's iconic law enforcement officers.

The accommodations at the Towne House certainly did not put it into the category of a five-star hotel. No sink, bathroom or shower in the room. You shared a communal bathroom and shower with other residents on the floor. My brother Ken moved into the Towne House at the same time that I did and had his own room. Neither of us had an issue in having to use communal bathrooms. I spent time on the oil fields living in a trailer that had no bathroom or kitchen. I also shared a communal bathroom at the fraternity house. Ken just spent a year in a forward base camp with outdoor latrines and showers.

The basic setup did not bother us since the rent was modest. We actually thought we were living large at the Towne House and had our own bar on the sixth floor, generally always packed with college-aged girls. Life was good.

I recall a night at the Towne House that started with one of the most embarrassing moments I have experienced before it turned into the greatest night of my life.

I left the Towne House for a date with a good-looking young lady, coincidentally from my neighborhood in Lorain. We had gone to different schools in Lorain and while we knew each other, we hadn't really talked nor dated. We met in a Psychology class at Kent, which was her major and perhaps gave her a better perception into my personality. I had dated many great-looking women before and unfortunately had an attitude of attempting to bed everyone that I dated. I started having sex with girls/women when I was 14. At dinner I guess I came on too strong as in the middle of dinner she got up, ended the date and loudly stated to all in the restaurant within earshot, that I should never attempt to call her again.

Sitting there somewhat embarrassed while the diners at other tables looked at me, I paid the check and headed back to the Towne House. Since it was still early, on my way home I stopped for a quick beer at the Cove Bar on Water Street. As I walked in, I spotted the most beautiful woman I had ever seen. I made my way through the crowd and introduced myself to the young lady whose name was Darlene Deem. She was with her girlfriend "Louie" and a young man who I later found out was Darlene's date that night.

I hung out with them, then went to a party at an upscale apartment complex at Kent, Tri-Towers. The rooms were crowded. Darlene walked out of the party and into the hallway. I walked out of the party and started talking with her. I took her to her dorm. All we did for hours was to sit in the student lounge downstairs and talk. We made a connection as though we were meant to cross paths that night. I realized then that this beautiful girl was someone I wanted to spend the rest of my life with. Darlene also met me at a time when I had lost my way, not only with women, but with my goals in life. She helped me to focus on becoming a better man.

The lesson I learned that night is that sometimes things happen for a reason. I could have retreated to the Towne House after getting rejected badly on my date earlier in the evening. Had I let that rejection take control over me I would have missed that once-in-a-lifetime opportunity to meet the woman who would become the love of my life, my best friend and future wife.

I met anti-war protestor Jerry Rupe at the Towne House. We became friends and talked a bit about the war protests and law enforcement, but generally just hung out from time to time. He was a nice guy who grew up in Ravenna. He was not the "Jerry Rubin" of Kent State. I never saw Jerry Rupe involved in any anti-war protest while I knew him.

I recall that he and I double dated, I took Darlene who I recently met, to see a new band that Jerry raved about. We went to see the Allman Brothers in Cleveland in 1971. This was the original Allman Brothers band with Duane and Greg Allman and Dickie Betts. Another great time in Cleveland, the home of Rock & Roll. It was an awesome show and my introduction to Southern Rock. Darlene and I still remember that concert every time we hear the song "In Memory of Elizabeth Reed" as we consider it one of "our songs." Every time I hear "Midnight Rider" I sadly think of Jerry Rupe since the lyrics portray a desperate man on the run. At the time Jerry was indicted and facing trial for his involvement in the May 2 evening protest at the ROTC building on the Kent campus.

I lost contact with Jerry after his sentencing for his involvement in the May 2 riots and never saw him again — another friend lost to the impact of the Viet Nam War.

Ron Deem (Darlene's brother), who I had not yet met but who would become my lifetime good friend and future brother-in-law, was a student in his second year at Kent State in the spring of 1970. He was on the way to class that infamous day when the National Guard opened fire on students. A sociology professor, Jerry Lewis, quickly instructed all of the students in his area to lay on the ground until the firing was over. That quick thinking by Professor Lewis, who would ultimately be my Social Theory professor, saved lives.

Ron told me that morning of May 4 he awoke to find a National Guard tank parked in the driveway of the house he and some friends rented that abutted the campus. He recalls seeing snipers on rooftops of various campus buildings while walking to class before and after the shooting. On that fateful day, he heard the sound of M1 rifles being fired. His first impression was that he thought it was fireworks.

Professor Lewis then instructed all the students in his immediate area to drop and lay flat on the ground. Ron's next impression once he realized it was rifle fire, was that these guardsmen fired indiscriminately in the crowd and emptied their clips into any one standing erect. He indicated that the firing seemed to last forever. The Guardsmen fired for 13 seconds, killing four students, permanently paralyzing another and wounding eight others.

Here is a description of what an M1 bullet can do to a human being: When an M1 bullet hits a human body, it creates a significant wound that destroys and rips tissue, causing a permanent cavity from the impact force. The striking power of this bullet often results in severe bleeding, organ damage, bone fractures and death.

Shooting students on the Kent State campus was our government's formal response to anti-war protests. The use of lethal force on U.S. citizens on a college campus was unprecedented. No students or civilians on campus fired any weapons. The threat to the National Guard was that some protestors may have been throwing stones. Firing your M1 into a group of unarmed students is not the proper or appropriate measure of force to be used in that situation.

A further abuse of crowd control tactics was the fact that the Ohio National Guard also advanced on the crowd with fixed bayonets. A fixed bayonet is not only a psychologically intimidating tactic, but in the event of any contact with the student protestors, the guardsmen would have a lethal weapon that would inflict severe injury to protestors, rather than using a less lethal force, such as a baton.

This was not an error in tactics. The guardsmen on campus were following direct orders to shoot to kill or severely injure protestors. Was this really the America that I grew up in?

My brother-in-law was back at his house as the guardsmen continued to disperse students, even after the shooting. Ron and his roommates recall a young protestor being chased by a National Guardsman and stabbed in the back on their front yard. Ron and his roommate carried the wounded student onto their porch for safety and called an ambulance. That student lost a kidney by that attack, literally being stabbed in the back by the marauding guardsman using indiscriminate force against students. A black day with the military acting as law enforcement. A black day for America.

Ron and his roommates could not get their cars out of their driveway for five days, the length of time the tank and occupying force of the Ohio National Guard were on campus. Ron asked one of the officers when the tank would be moved. Ron was advised that the tank would be moved, "when the command came down to move that tank," and until then it would remain in place, even though it blocked the driveway preventing the tenants from removing their vehicles. The officer in charge told my future brother-in-law that, *"if any of you hippies think about writing "Pig" on the tank, I will have you shot."*

Ron was not a hippie. He was a very good high school athlete and son of a great Ohio high school football coach, Ron Deem, Sr. voted one year as Ohio High School Coach of the Year. Ron was in pre-law and would become an accomplished attorney and entrepreneur in the oil and gas business in Ohio and West Virginia. To the officer in charge, Ron was not a fellow American but was looked down upon with the utter disdain shown to all the Kent State students by the Ohio National Guard.

That was the tense environment of the Kent campus over that five-day period. Essentially, the Kent campus was under martial law with all civil rights suspended. This was an unprecedented military response to unarmed civil protests on a college campus. Another terrible stain on our society and a reflection of the response of the military industrial complex to a national movement to oppose an endless war that had no direction.

The Viet Nam War itself was a fraud. It was initiated under false pretenses based upon a claimed attack on the U.S. Navy by Viet Nam patrol boats.

President Johnson in what seemed to be one of his first acts as President, seized on the false narrative in advancing the Gulf of Tonkin resolution to declare all-out war on Viet Nam. Keep in mind, the U.S. Navy in 1964 was considered the most powerful navy in the world. By comparison, the North Vietnamese Navy, also known as the Vietnam People's Navy (PVN), was considered to be a relatively small naval force, primarily consisting of a few dozen torpedo boats, with the most notable engagement against the U.S. Navy involving three P-4 class torpedo boats.

The Gulf of Tonkin incident became Johnson's excuse to launch a massive, endless war in Viet Nam. This was Johnson's *"weapons of mass destruction"* excuse to embroil the United States into a major war with no plan for victory other than for massive profits by the military industrial complex.

The fall of 1970 was not much different, other than there was no occupation by the National Guard. However, there was always a strong sense of a military/law enforcement presence. Armed riot police walking the streets of downtown Kent occurred a lot, especially at night. While on a date with Darlene and while walking down Main Street in downtown Kent, we saw a large, unmarked bus carrying a full load of riot police who were bent over in their seats to avoid detection. They were deployed on Water Street to march on students assembled in groups outside some of the bars.

On another occasion, I recall coming out of the Cove Bar on Water Street and heard the bullhorn of the leader of a large riot squad of police announcing that those people on the street standing around had to disperse. We were not protesting. No signs or banners were being waived. We were standing there talking. Perhaps someone was smoking a joint but no activity that resembled any type of protest. Just the opposite. We were enjoying a night on the town in America.

I was standing in that crowd after a set by one of the bands that often played the club. They often included Joe Walsh and the James Gang, Eric Carmen and the Raspberries, among others. Side note on Eric Carmen: I was at their show another night with Darlene and recall that during a break he wanted to hit on Darlene since she was the best-looking girl in the club. He frequently but unsuccessfully tried to call to date her. So I'm not a big Eric Carmen and the Raspberries fan and don't have fond memories when I hear their song "Go All The Way."

As I was standing there that night I was not with Darlene. All of us on Water Street were ordered to disperse promptly when again we were just enjoying ourselves and legally, as granted to us by the U.S. Constitution, simply "peacefully assembling." Everyone I saw there was relaxing and hanging out. I knew that I was not protesting anything nor was that even the subject of any conversations I heard. Yet the riot police began marching shoulder-to-shoulder spread wide across Water Street from storefront to storefronts so that no one could evade them. This was a common event and you had to know where the riot police were to your rear or on your flanks to plan your escape.

I understood how the riot squad deployed from my classroom studies on crowd control and how they at times attempted to set up on the flanks and perimeters to capture student protestors. I determined the route to evade this riot squad sweep and ran to avoid confrontation by taking an alleyway between the streets. No chance an officer would be able to catch me under any circumstances and absolutely no chance since some were wearing heavy riot gear. I was fast enough to avoid being swept up in that unnecessary show of force to break up a crowd of students trying to enjoy an evening on the town. Others were not so fortunate. That was the reality of student life at Kent State during those tumultuous years.

My brother Ken recalls being at the Robin Hood bar close to campus for happy hour on May 4, 1971, the first anniversary of the May 4 shooting. When Ken left the bar, it was dark. The riot police, apparently anticipating demonstrations, had set up a mortar position in the middle of the intersection in front of the Robin Hood at East Main and Lincoln, across from the Kent campus.

As Ken walked out of the Robin Hood, he observed riot police launching flares over the Kent campus. Ken told me when he saw that he immediately started to think of flashbacks to Viet Nam. The flares were being sent up to light up the skies for law enforcement to be able to spot and arrest protestors. The police had their own war against anti-Viet Nam protestors, that war being waged on the Kent campus.

During that same time period, Ken and I took a class titled Traffic and Riot/Crowd Control as part of our criminal justice curriculum.

Our professor advised the class we would have a field trip the next night and to meet on the Kent commons. He advised us to bring a wet towel or handkerchief to the field trip. We did not know why, but soon found out.

We set up our field trip classroom on campus positioned to observe riot squad members with grenade launchers preparing to fire tear gas canisters to disperse the crowd gathering on the commons. Our professor spoke to law enforcement and pre-arranged our observation area, making sure we were positioned just right. He notified law enforcement in advance that this particular group of students were observing their training to become members of law enforcement.

My brother Ken, after graduating, went to work for the Dade County Sheriff's department in Florida in the Criminal Investigation Division. He wanted to join the Dade County Sheriff's office at the time because the homicide rate in Miami was the highest in the country. Plenty of activity if you were an action junkie.

Our professor provided his field trip class with a running narrative of the law enforcement tactics of how the riot police set up. Riot police determined the direction the wind was blowing in relation to the protestors and determined what location to lob tear gas canisters. The strategy and tactics were to fire the canisters to land and explode upwind of the protestors so that when the canisters detonated, the wind would carry the tear gas into the crowd to maximize the effectiveness of the tear gas on the protestors.

Our classroom on riot and crowd control was the actual campus and our fellow protesting students were the targets of the riot squad's dispersal tactics that we were being taught. The course study chapter on protestors and riot police jumped off the printed page of our textbooks as we were watching and learning crowd control in real time right in front of our faces. A surreal college learning experience for a pre-law student. I felt like a stranger in a strange land.

As an aside, I never was pepper sprayed or suffered tear gas in those anti-war protests since I never participated in any student protests. At the time of observing the riot police, I never experienced what tear gas felt like as I watched these demonstrations of riot control on our campus.

However, I did not escape the sting of tear gas. On the night before the Fourth of July in 1972, I did attend a Rod Stewart concert at the Akron Rubber Bowl. I was not working security, rather I was on a date with Darlene.

The opening acts that night were Badfinger and Cactus. While we were in the stands enjoying the show, the riot police at the Rubber Bowl fired tear gas on a group trying to crash the gate directly outside the stadium close to our seating area.

Poor tactics by the riot police coupled with a strong wind entering the Rubber Bowl caused the tear gas intended for the gate crashers to waft in and over sections of the Rubber Bowl including our section.

The effect of tear gas is debilitating once you inhale the gas, sending a burning sensation to your lungs as well as your eyes and nose. Darlene and I had to scramble to get to the bathrooms to wash our faces from that tear gas. That gave me firsthand experience as to what those protestors on campus dealt with when they were tear gassed. It was not a fun experience.

For me it was another Fourth of July event at a football stadium that ended in a lot of physical discomfort, following my beat down several years earlier at George Daniel Field in Lorain.

I made a mental note never to attend a Fourth of July event at a stadium in the future.

CLOSING ARGUMENT

CHAPTER 25

Reconciling
What I Learned

REVISITING THE HISTORICAL SETTING
BEFORE JFK's ASSASSINATION

My interview with Joseph G. Helmich has weighed heavily on me over the years.

Reflecting back on that day at the prison in Alabama, reviewing the *KAK: Manuscript* too many times and considering all the information I have compiled over the years on this topic, this project was important for me to share with the world. For me, for my generation, for my children's and grandchildren's generations and for the greater good of all Americans I feel it is important to share the information I have.

The 1960s in America - and throughout the world - were turbulent times. And sharing the allegations made by Helmich, hopefully sheds new light on the mysterious assassination of John F. Kennedy.

Also by highlighting the resultant sacrifices that our fighting men and women endured as a direct result of decisions made by the U.S. Government to initiate a massive war in Viet Nam, a war which might have never been had Kennedy lived, is my way of honoring their heroism.

By using my own viewpoint as a young man in America living

through these times, I've tried to provide a glimpse into the upheaval that my generation went through as a result of the Kennedy Assassination. I wanted to reconcile historical information with the information from my interview with Helmich and his manuscript to make sense of what I learned.

My view of our country dramatically changed after interviewing Helmich that hot summer day in Talladega. The clouded suspicion that I previously had about the Kennedy Assassination became so clear after getting to see behind the curtain of these dramatic events.

I am reminded of that interview with Helmich every time I hear the lyrics to the Eric Church song "Talladega." To me, this song rings true. From that summer day forward, my eyes were opened to the real world in America, a society in large part controlled by a powerful group of unelected individuals and government organizations which make decisions and plot the future course of our country.

I tried to concisely explain my review and analysis of what I learned from reading Helmich's manuscript, information that I was previously prevented from releasing due to threats from my own government. To do so, it is important to frame all the events in the historical setting in which they took place.

At the time of my interview with Helmich, I had heard the phrase, *"military industrial complex,"* which President Dwight D. Eisenhower warned about in his farewell speech from the White House on January 17, 1961.

It's ironic that the retiring President of the United States and former Supreme Allied Commander in the victorious campaigns in Europe and, later, as the Chief of Staff of the Armed Forces had alerted all of us - and perhaps incoming President Kennedy specifically - about the growth and power of the military and the defense industry.

I was not aware of the term "Deep State" at the time. One accepted definition of the "Deep State" is: "an alleged secret network of non-elected government officials and sometimes private entities (as in the financial services and defense industries) operating extralegally to influence and enact government policy."

If speaking today, Eisenhower could easily substitute *"Deep State"* for the *military industrial complex* as part of his warning to all of us in his farewell address.

To put this in context, U.S. Military spending is a major business in America. It was reported that in only the first half of 2023, defense contractors and other defense sector players spent nearly $70 million just in lobbying the federal government for a half year. Much of this lobbying concerned the 2024 National Defense Authorization Act, an annual appropriations bill funding the Pentagon and military operations. The fiscal year 2024 (FY2024) presidential budget request was $842 billion. The annual military budget in the United States dwarfs the total GDP of many of the countries in the world.

The United States spends more on its military than the next nine countries combined and that includes China, Russia and India among others.

When addressing the military industrial complex or the Deep State, that is one powerful entity, operating a major world business generating billions in profits. It makes you wonder, who controls the military industrial complex? And who has that awesome power?

Inevitably with that amount of power comes corruption.

"Power tends to corrupt and absolute power corrupts absolutely," said Lord Acton. "Great men are almost always bad men, even when they exercise influence and not authority; still more when you superadd the tendency of the certainty of corruption by authority."

I prefer the more noble saying that, *"with great power comes great responsibility,"* but that quality seems rare in politicians of any era.

As individual citizens, how can we require that those exercising that power are guided by the sense of morality that this country was founded upon and that those entrusted with that power accept such responsibility to guide America? How as individuals can we voice our opposition to the Deep State if those actions run afoul of the principles America was founded on?

From my perspective, one way is to shine a light on what we know and what needs to be revealed and corrected. We can do that by speaking up and making sure that it is well known that there remain patriots on both sides of the aisle representing both parties having in their hearts the best interest of our country. Even if only one voice from one citizen, we need to address that power and call out any abuses that we see taking place.

My voice and that call out is contained in this book. Although there is no record of him saying it, Kennedy is credited with the phrase, *"One person can make a difference and everyone should try."* That has never been truer.

Since that summer I met Joe Helmich and read his manuscript; I have wanted to be that one voice to call out what Helmich alleged and what I believed occurred in 1963. As I explain in this book, these events allowed for the endless Viet Nam War to start and continue. That war cost the lives of my friends, affected my generation and forever changed America.

The U.S. Department of Justice initially blocked me from releasing Helmich's manuscript by its cease-and-desist letter. Time has passed and circumstances have changed. I now want to speak up to share with my children and my grandchildren, as well as their generations, the information that was revealed to me. A lesson may be learned by them. Perhaps they also can recognize that they need to be that one voice, that one person speaking up in defense of our country. Such action on their part will make a difference.

To make sense of these events and information, it is important to recognize the time period and events leading up to Nov. 22, 1963. To frame the issues for evaluating the potential evidence to support a conspiracy to assassinate Kennedy, I wanted to briefly frame the 15 or so years before Kennedy was assassinated to look at the historical context of the time leading up to the assassination.

During that time period, I also point to Joseph G. Helmich's rapid rise through the ranks over a 10-year period to become an army warrant officer and crypto custodian holding the highest security clearance issued by our military. Helmich's role as a crypto custodian encompassed the responsibility for the *"custody, handling, safeguarding and destruction of code making materials."*

Here is the historical setting leading up to Kennedy's Assassination:

1938 to 1940

Signed on Sept. 30, 1938, by Britain, France, Germany and Italy, *The Munich Agreement* allowed Germany to annex the Sudetenland, a border region of Czechoslovakia with a large German population. Essentially, the world handed over a good portion of the now Czech Republic to Hitler as a sacrificial offering.

For context, President Kennedy's father, Joseph Kennedy, was then ambassador to Great Britain before World War II. He favored appeasement of the Nazis and Hitler. Joseph Kennedy joined with Great Britain's Prime Minister, Neville Chamberlain, in this appeasement effort before World War II to maintain peace in response to Nazi aggression.

The appeasement strategy was a colossal failure and did nothing to prevent World War II.

The naivete of those leaders when facing a world threat allowed for the Third Reich's ascension. That rise of evil was hidden in plain sight of our leaders. All they had to do was read Hitler's *Mein Kampf.*

1939 to 1945

World War II, a global conflict between the Allies and the Axis powers, raged throughout the world with 56 countries engaged in the conflict. Many nations mobilized their resources in pursuit of total war. World War II, the deadliest conflict in history, resulted in an estimated 70 to 85 million deaths.

1948

The Soviets, in what might be considered the trigger to the Cold War, initiated the Blockade of Berlin resulting in a massive airlift and the start of major tensions between the United States and the Soviets.

The rise of communism and the socialist society started in Russia and expanded with the creation of the Soviet Union. The

Soviets spread this infectious and evil concept throughout the world. The Cold War and all its underlying issues lasted until the collapse of the Soviet Union in 1991.

1949

The U.S. joined the North Atlantic Treaty Organization (NATO) to form the first global military alliance in U.S. history. That same year, the Communist regime took over after a brutal civil war in China costing the lives of an estimated 1 million to 2 million people. China then joined forces with the Soviets to create a massive Communist front.

China had the largest population in the world. The Soviet Union had the largest country in the world geographically. Those countries ramped up world domination and did so as nuclear powers. The following year, communist North Korea invaded South Korea. The world now recognized that after defeating Nazi Germany and then the militant Empire of Japan, we faced possibly even larger, more powerful and, if possible, more brutal and evil enemies than the Nazis. These were troubling times.

This remains historically relevant. Note the potential new axis of power: Russia, China, Iran and North Korea. That is a new world danger. We must remember our history.

1952

Former General Dwight D. Eisenhower, at one time Commander of all U.S. and Allied Forces in World War II, is elected President of the United States. The Republican served two terms until 1960. Eisenhower's vice president? Richard Nixon.

1954

Helmich enlisted in the U.S. Army. He served two years in Korea. Helmich was an American Soldier when he started his career.

1958

Helmich received training and obtained top-secret clearance at the Signal Training Center in Fort Gordon, Georgia - now called Fort Eisenhower - and was then assigned to the U.S. Communications Zone Europe in Orleans, France.

1959

Helmich is assigned to the 275th Signal Company in Paris. Within a few years Helmich will be appointed warrant officer, holding top-secret clearance and working as a custodian for classified cryptologic documents.

Fall of 1960

John Kennedy, a Democrat, narrowly defeated Nixon to become President of the United States in a close and bitter election that was too close to call until the following day.

In Illinois, there were rampant rumors that Chicago's Mayor Richard Daley used his political machine to stuff the ballot box in Cook County for Kennedy. Democrats charged the GOP with similar tactics in southern Illinois.

Down in Texas, there were similar claims about the influence of Kennedy's running mate, Lyndon B. Johnson, over that state's election and rampant assertions of election fraud and voter interference. Kennedy defeated Nixon with 56.4 percent of the Electoral College and 49.72 percent of the popular vote. Nixon, who won more states, received 49.55 percent of the popular vote. A close and bitter Presidential election with overtones of election interference. Sound familiar? That is how the Kennedy presidency started.

January 17, 1961

President Eisenhower gives his Farewell Address to the Nation. In that speech, he warns of the military industrial complex.

April 17 to April 19, 1961

Three months after Eisenhower's Farewell Address, the United States, without Congressional authority, sponsors an invasion of Cuba with anti-Castro Cuban exiles trained by the CIA. To reduce the explicit link with U.S. Military assistance, Kennedy chose not to authorize U.S. air strikes. The invasion failed spectacularly. This was commonly called the Bay of Pigs Invasion. A major black eye for America and a pivotal event in Kennedy's presidency.

September 25, 1961

Kennedy, in a dramatic and moving address to the United Nations General Assembly, warned of the weapons of mass destruction now being stockpiled and proposed complete world disarmament. Some of his words from that address:

> "...Men no longer debate whether armaments are a symptom or a cause of tension. The mere existence of modern weapons – ten million times more powerful than any that the world has ever seen, and only minutes away from any target on earth – is a source of horror, and discord and distrust. Men no longer maintain that disarmament must await the settlement of all disputes – for disarmament must be a part of any permanent settlement. And men may no longer pretend that the quest for disarmament is a sign of weakness - for in a spiraling arms race, a nation's security may well be shrinking even as its arms increase."

President Kennedy's desire for world peace, viewed through the lens of our war hawkish military leaders at the time, could have been considered as the coming of the second great appeasement strategy to the new World Bully — Marxist and Leninist communism.

Many military leaders believed at the time, and perhaps rightly so, that appeasement in the face of worldwide dominance sought by the communist would fail just as appeasement advocated by Kennedy's father did with the Nazis.

From an American military hardliner viewpoint, the election of Kennedy and his desire for world peace, may have been viewed as a far less than appropriate message to send in those dangerous times. The repeated requests for peace by Kennedy were viewed by many as more Pollyanna than pragmatic. U.S. Military hardliners asserted that worldwide communist aggression, perhaps rightly so, needed to be met with a show of force. Their attitude was more the "Fighting Sons of Sparta" than the idealistic "Messenger of Peace" that was Kennedy.

Late 1961

Helmich is appointed to the rank of warrant officer. A warrant officer in the United States Army is a highly trained, specialized expert who serves as a technical leader.

Warrant officers are often promoted from enlisted ranks for their technical expertise. In Helmich's case, his new rank went well with his top-secret security clearance designation and the responsibility for the custody, handling, safeguarding and destruction of code making materials.

Fall of 1962

The Soviet Union began to secretly install missiles in Cuba to launch attacks on U.S. cities. This was not recognized by our CIA or military intelligence until after the intercontinental ballistic missiles were armed and ready to launch at the U.S. The confrontation that followed, known as the Cuban Missile Crisis, brought the two superpowers to the brink of war before an agreement was reached to withdraw the missiles.

This crisis was resolved by negotiations Kennedy led, but the hardliners felt that America should have done more to address the Soviet Union's expansion into the Western Hemisphere.

Fall of 1962

In Helmich's manuscript, he vividly identifies that he was responsible for sending, receiving and deciphering ominous military intelligence traffic putting America on the doorstep of World War III due to the Cuban Missile Crisis.

Early 1963

Helmich is recruited, as he advised me in our interview, and as he identifies in his manuscript, by a CIA agent to act as a CIA operative. Helmich told me he was taught detailed spycraft, initially to establish his backstory to convince the Soviets as to his motivation to release classified information.

Helmich began his spycraft training and built his backstory of a desperate soldier in need of a loan due to passing two bad checks. He employed this spycraft training for a period of 17 years. He worked inside and outside the military as well as on missions within and outside the United States, where he engaged in various assignments.

In 1963, Helmich began a well-rehearsed presentation at the Soviet Embassy in Paris, and offered to sell them military secrets over the course of the next year.

June 10, 1963

President John F. Kennedy arrived on the campus of American University in our nation's capital to deliver a commencement speech that would change the course of history. Kennedy laid out his own vision for world peace in his famous address:

> *"What kind of a peace do I mean and what kind of a peace do we seek? Not a Pax Americana enforced on the world by American weapons of war. Not the peace of the grave or the security of the slave.*

I am talking about genuine peace – the kind of peace that makes life on earth worth living; the kind that enables men and nations to grow and to hope and to build a better life for their children. Not merely peace for Americans but peace for all men and women; not merely peace in our time but peace in all time."

A moving speech that seemed to be an achievable goal of world peace. From the date of that speech, Kennedy had a little more than five months to live.

Summer of 1963

Helmich solidified a relationship with the GRU, the Soviet Military Intelligence, and began providing the information on the KL-7 cryptograph machine, the key component of U.S. secret intelligence communications. He is transferred stateside to Fort Bragg, N.C., where he continues in his top-secret position and has access to our top military codes.

Fall of 1963

Helmich is directed by his alleged CIA handler to be prepared to travel to Paris sometime in late November to deliver updated military coding and other materials to the Soviets.

October 11, 1963

National Security Action Memorandum Number 263 (NSAM-263) was a national security directive approved by President Kennedy. It identified that 1,000 military personnel could be withdrawn from South Vietnam by the end of 1963, and that a "major part of the U.S. Military task can be completed by the end of 1965."

Kennedy essentially announced we would be withdrawing troops from Viet Nam. Kennedy has six weeks to live.

November 11, 1963

President Ngô Đình Diệm and the Personalist Labor Revolutionary Party of the Republic of Vietnam (South Vietnam) were deposed by the CIA-backed Army of the Republic of Vietnam officers.

This was a major coup d'etat in which the CIA played a significant role less than two weeks before Kennedy was assassinated. President Diệm was captured and executed the next day, along with his brother and advisor Ngô Đình Nhu for a complete regime change in South Viet Nam. This is believed to be one of many CIA-led regime changes in the world during the mid-20th century.

November 22, 1963

Helmich, after receiving instructions from his alleged CIA handler, traveled to Paris, accompanied by his wife Jean, so he could complete his mission and provide the Soviets with U.S. Military key codes. This transaction would allow the Soviets to decipher current coded messages over the KL-7, which Helmich already had provided the Soviets.

Meanwhile, Kennedy landed at Love Field in Dallas, Texas for a prearranged speech. This will be his last day on Earth.

While en route to New York for his connecting flight to Paris, Helmich and his wife, Jean, hear the pilot's announcement of Kennedy's assassination. After landing in New York, Helmich contacted his handler to confirm instructions and is advised he is to immediately proceed to Paris to conclude his mission.

Over the next day, Helmich delivered all of the key codes to the KL-7 to enable the Soviet GRU to decipher U.S. top-secret military intelligence to determine whether the United States would retaliate against the Soviet Union for Kennedy's assassination. By deciphering U.S. communications, the Soviets learned that no such retaliation was ever considered.

These facts identify - and Helmich's allegations corroborate - that there appeared to be knowledge in advance for this major event to take place on Nov. 22, 1963. If Helmich is to be believed, he played a major role in a well-thought-out plot to assassinate the then-sitting President of the United States.

These actions not only changed world history, but had a specific and direct effect on my generation growing up at the start of the Viet Nam War. The deaths of many of my childhood friends would soon begin.

CHAPTER 26

Ukrainian Heritage

MY BACKGROUND PROVIDES ODD CONNECTION TO ANOTHER SENSELESS WAR

The nuns kidding me about my initials *KFJ* being the reverse of *JFK's* initials was not the only time my name had some significance.

Many years later, I learned something more ironic about my name while having a conversation with another client of mine, retired General James Dozier. I represented him in presenting his story on his abduction by the terrorist group Red Brigade.

Gen. Dozier asked me if I knew the origin of my last name. I told him that I knew that my grandfather emigrated from Krakow, Poland, and my last name was previously spelled differently, but not much more than that.

Gen. Dozier went on to tell me that Felix Edmundovich Dzerzhinsky was a Polish-born Bolshevik revolutionary and politician.

From 1917 until his death in 1926, he led the first two Soviet secret police organizations, the Cheka and the OGPU, and was credited as being the founder of the forerunner of the KGB.

The pronunciation of Dzerzhinsky (d-ZHER-zhin-ski or d-ZER-zhin-ski) is the exact pronunciation of my last name Jursinski, which previously was phonetically spelled Jurczynsky and other derivations by immigration officials.

Gen. Dozier inquired as to whether Felix Edmundovich Dzerzhinsky was a relative. He was surprised that I was unaware that my last name was the same or pronounced the same as the founder of the Soviet intelligence agencies.

The fact that my last name had the same pronunciation as the founder of the KGB and that founder was Polish was disconcerting. I have wondered if that could be part of my heritage.

I was Polish on my father's side. On my mother's side, my grandfather and grandmother were from the plains of the Ukraine where they emigrated to work in the steel town I grew up in. They were of Russian Orthodox faith and hated the Soviets for what they did to Ukraine during the 1930s, starving millions of Ukrainians.

In what has become known as the *Holodomor*, it was the first genocide that was methodically planned out and perpetrated by depriving the Ukrainian people of food that they produced. This was the first example of iron-fisted government control by a communist state.

Scholars point out that between 3.5 to 7 million Ukrainians were starved to death. They also note that it was especially horrific withholding food as a weapon of genocide and that it was done in a region of the world known as the "Breadbasket of Europe." Reflect on that as you consider the Ukrainian war with Russia that began in 2022.

My mother explained to me that this was one reason her parents left Ukraine to journey to America. Their hatred of the Soviets can be easily discerned from the quote many attribute to Joseph Stalin when asked about millions of Ukrainians starving in the Holodomor. Stalin's utterly soulless statement was: "One death is a tragedy; a million deaths is a statistic."

My Ukrainian heritage taught me to hate the communist regime. led by the Russian Soviets. I have a good friend and colleague, Attorney Tom Fricke, who also is Ukrainian. During the Viet Nam War, Tom sacrificed the opportunity to immediately start law school and instead enlisted in the U.S. Army. Tom was an American Soldier.

Being Ukrainian and due to the modern war in Ukraine with the Russians, Tom recently sent me the Ukrainian fighting slogan: "*Slava Ukraini*," which translates to "*Glory to Ukraine!*" It is a national salute and battle cry that symbolizes Ukrainian sovereignty and resistance to foreign aggression.

War Still Rages On

Notwithstanding my ingrained hatred of the Soviet communist regime due to my Ukrainian heritage, I am conflicted as to what appears to be another endless war fueled by U.S. tax dollars, which is having a detrimental impact on American citizens.

While I am of Ukrainian descent on my mother's side, I am first and foremost an American concerned with the best interest of my country.

While I have hatred of the Russians in my DNA, I have concerns as to the massive amount of funds being sent by America to Ukraine with no real accountability. All of the statistics show that in dollars contributed, the U.S. has sent almost as much monetary aid to Ukraine as all of the other NATO allies combined.

The money the U.S. has given to Ukraine is equal to the entire annual military budget in Afghanistan. The transfer of this enormous amount of money with no accounting of the funds or control given to Ukraine is troubling.

Ukraine has been objectively identified as one of the more corrupt countries on the planet. Its ranking is No. 105 out of the 180 most corrupt countries in the world as rated by the Corruption Perception Index. [26-1]

Why is America contributing disproportionately when the immediacy of the threat is to those European countries? This amount being paid to the Ukrainian government does not include the weapon systems and equipment being provided, which even further tips the scales against the United States.

Making matters worse, Ukraine has imposed martial law and has taken away the freedoms of its people. Under martial law, the government and the military leadership in Ukraine have the right to restrict the freedom of movement of citizens as well as confiscate private or communal property for state needs. Isn't government confiscation of property rights and restriction of free speech what communists do?

Who is profiting from what undoubtedly are funds being syphoned off since there appears to be no true accounting? Why are we not using U.S. influence to find a resolution to the conflict? It begs the question as to why we did not avoid the invasion to start with.

This same theme of protracted and endless war that has developed over the past two decades where the military industrial complex advocates for heavy military expenditures, continues with no clear objectives for peace. And in this case for a country not even a member of NATO, when the U.S. national debt exceeds a staggering $36 trillion.

Is this yet another endless war to enable the military industrial complex to profit vs. efforts on resolution?

With the suggested corruption and graft in Ukraine, are there individuals and entities in Ukraine and elsewhere that cheer on the continuation of the war only because of the profits being made? And the more damage to Ukraine, the more aid will be needed if this war ever ends to rebuild Ukraine.

Can America continue to foot the bill for the war and the anticipated costs to rebuild Ukraine by printing more money that results in higher inflation, all to fuel enormous profits flowing to the military industrial complex? Will the American people continue to get saddled with debt and feel the impact of increased inflation if we have to continue to pay for this war?

Seems a pattern is clearly developing - in plain sight - that has resulted in massive expenditures by the U.S. Government when issues in America need attention. While the U.S. defends the security of Ukraine due to an invasion across its borders, we had the Biden Administration, at the same time disregard the invasion across the U.S. borders, north and south, which has a security impact on our own country and citizens.

I find it ironic that with the background of my Polish name and Ukrainian heritage, that I of all people was entrusted with the information on Soviet espionage linking it to one of the biggest stories in American history through my meeting with Joseph G. Helmich. And that the broader story reflects upon a more pervasive theme of control in world history by the military industrial complex.

26-1: The Corruption Perceptions Index from Transparency International, a global coalition against corruption (https://www.transparency.org/en/cpi/2024).

CHAPTER 27

The Reality In America

THE DEEP STATE EXISTS, HIDDEN IN PLAIN SIGHT

I pray all of the classified files on the Kennedy Assassination will be fully released and without all of the redactions that I observed in the FBI's declassification of the file on Helmich. President Donald Trump has made this a focus of his second term, and at the time of publishing this book what we have been told is that all of the information on Kennedy has been released. I wonder if those files have been sanitized like the declassified files I have obtained on *Operation Hook Shot?*

Will the release of the declassified files actually name names and identify the perpetrators? This information needs to be considered by the many generations who did not experience the Kennedy Assassination firsthand as this event remains a painful memory to so many of my generation. There is some hope that the U.S. Government will finally reveal to us what actually happened. So far, we have not been told the truth.

The lesson I learned from reflecting on the Helmich interview and manuscript, as well as everything that I have read or viewed about the Kennedy Assassination, is there was a clear reason why Kennedy was killed and by whom. I have carried these thoughts with me for more than 40 years.

From my perspective, it appears clear that President Johnson and the military industrial complex initiated a full-out engagement and claimed that they would vigorously escalate the Viet Nam War. Johnson, as Commander in Chief, ordered the deployment of far too many of our finest young men and women into harm's way to meet their fate. In total, approximately 3 million American Soldiers would be deployed to Southeast Asia.

There would be more than $100 billion spent on the Viet Nam War. That would be about $500 billion today. Big business and big profits for the military industrial complex.

My belief is shared by many others that Kennedy would have never allowed the Viet Nam War to expand in that manner. We can only wonder what would have been America's direction had he lived to fulfill all those dreams for our country and the world that he articulated?

Kennedy's strategy toward his objective of world peace was deemed a threat to America by certain unnamed and unelected leaders. Kennedy was removed because he posed a threat to the buildup for the Viet Nam War.

I believe that Kennedy's actions and announced goals for world peace and disarmament were perceived by some as a clear and present danger to the United States. I also believe he was perceived to be an existential threat to the security of our country, and specifically a major threat to the military industrial complex and the CIA.

The facts support Kennedy's removal by force far more than the story fed to us that one man alone pulled the trigger.

The violent and brutal assassination of Kennedy for all the world to see may have also been a message that the Deep State was sending out to assert its control. When Kennedy was removed, it plunged my generation into a perilous time, designed in part to generate massive profits for the military industrial complex and the Deep State.

I want this book to provide information and additional evidence on the Kennedy Assassination from what I have learned from my interview with Joseph G. Helmich, my review of his manuscript and the transcript of his criminal trial. The unrefuted events that occurred on Nov. 22, 1963 involving Joseph G. Helmich supported the proposition that without question a group of powerful individuals and organizations knew in advance what was to take place that fateful day in Dallas.

With this evidence, I hope future generations will learn from the past and apply it to what is unfolding around them and what may happen in the future. All American citizens need to open their eyes.

This book is a look back at an impactful event in American history that layers into the story new revelations from Joseph Helmich that were buried. It is not a critique on criminal trial skills nor another conspiracy theory novel.

It is not an attack on our military leaders or on the general goals of our intelligence agencies. It was not written to second guess the good faith efforts of some of our leaders in America at the time. It certainly is not meant to critique the strategy and tactics of U.S. Military leaders who fought bravely besides the American Soldiers that served under them.

I simply want to point out that the convenient and spoon-fed assassination theory provided to us by governmental officials does not add up nor should it be believed in light of the facts as viewed analytically with the evidence we have to date. When applying the information that I have seen and reviewed, the planned espionage activities of Helmich culminated on Nov. 22-23, 1963. His travel to Paris the day of and turnover of top-secret codes the day after the assassination of Kennedy supports the fact that a group of individuals or organizations had prior knowledge of the plan.

Helmich himself was portrayed in the media as yet another lone-wolf traitor who somehow got around all of the top-secret security protections to remove highly classified and critical information to turn it over to Soviet military intelligence.

Similar circumstances surrounded Helmich as it did Lee Harvey Oswald. Oswald was purportedly a lone-wolf gunman who somehow evaded and circumvented all our security measures. The relaxation of some of the security measures around Kennedy I term *"planned negligence."*

The security surrounding Kennedy is also oddly similar to the purported lone-wolf gunman, Thomas Matthew Crooks, who somehow evaded all security protections when he was afforded the opportunity to take the kill shot on President Donald Trump at a campaign stop in Butler, Pennsylvania. Crooks' attempted assassination was in plain sight, for all of us to see except for those on the security team apparently charged with Trump's actual protection. Was this security lapse the result of *planned negligence*, just as the Kennedy assassination was the result of lax security protocols designed to set up his assassination?

Were the massive security failures involving the assassination attempt on Trump just a coincidence like the documented relaxation of security and protocol for the protection of Kennedy in Dallas on Nov. 22, 1963? Or was there some organization that allowed these security lapses to occur?

In both the Kennedy Assassination and the attempted assassination of Trump, the lone-wolf assassin was hidden in plain sight and afforded every opportunity to succeed given the divergence from standard security measures, eerily similar in pattern in both instances.

I wonder if history is repeating itself in the actions of the Secret Service and our intelligence agencies in not releasing information on the current assassination attempts on President Trump's life, by both Thomas Matthew Crookes and Ryan Wesely Routh the same way it was held back on Oswald? This lack of transparency by our intelligence agencies has been objected to by both Republicans and Democrats. This is not a Republican or Democratic dispute. Both sides of the political aisle want answers for the good of America.

Again, why are these agencies not accountable to Congressional oversight? And why are they continuing to block the release of information demanded by both parties in Congress?

This book should relieve all of us of the notion that Kennedy was a one-off murder by an individual who just happened to kill the President of the United States with no apparent motive or coordination by others.

"Great world events don't occur by happenstance," as Helmich told me in our interview. Helmich also told me that he was taught the phrase by his CIA handlers that, "Coincidence is the word we use when we can't see the levers and pulleys." Someday soon, we may all see the "levers and pulleys" behind the orchestrated assassination of our 35th President.

The well-thought-out assassination of Kennedy set off massive military spending on an endless war in Viet Nam.

It took an enormous toll on our country and society by the blood and treasure expended. More than 58,000 soldiers died. It directly inflicted significant pain on my generation. The cost was incalculable to our national psyche. The War Machine profited. The Deep State was satiated.

This is the recurring theme over the last 60 years reflecting America's war efforts from Viet Nam to the decades-old wars in Afghanistan and Iraq. Whether it was a Democratic or Republican administration, there has always been the pursuit of endless wars. Throughout these conflicts, the heroic American Soldier was used as the instrument for these wars.

There also was the one common factor former President Eisenhower warned of in his farewell speech on Jan. 17, 1961. Three days before Kennedy took office, Eisenhower said:

> *"We must never let the weight of this combination endanger our liberties or democratic processes. We should take nothing for granted. Only an alert and knowledgeable citizenry can compel the proper meshing of the huge industrial and military machinery of defense with our peaceful methods and goals, so that security and liberty may prosper together."*

Eisenhower's concerns were justified. The military industrial complex has relished the big war and the massive expenditure of funds that generated obscene profit for all those involved. The Deep State should take a bow for running such a profitable business.

Regardless, the actions taken by these yet-named organizations to remove a sitting President as their political enemy is not authority granted to these organizations by the U.S. Constitution or to any government intelligence agency. Such actions are not theirs to take. America is "a nation of laws" and everyone is to be governed by the same laws, regardless of their station.

Our constitutional government has safeguards in place identifying the manner and method our citizens can use to address grievances with public officials. It is by the ballot box. Self-help by a secret group of powerful but unelected officials is not what the U.S. Constitution contemplated.

Removal of your opponent by assassination, real or political, based upon the belief that it is justified due to some group's belief that the opponent poses a clear and present danger to our country is not how our or any government was designed to work.

For a nameless few to advance their own agenda, no matter how much justification they can claim, abuses the power given them as representatives of the U.S. Government. To fully resolve the Kennedy Assassinaton riddle, one must ask the cynical questions:

Who profited from Kennedy's assassination?

Who benefitted by the start of the seemingly endless Viet Nam War and the massive investment of blood and treasure?

Focus now on the present: Each year a new adversary to the United States or one of our allies is identified. Each year a new enemy is targeted. A new war is needed to be waged. Does this all serve our national interest? And is this what America was founded upon? We see these events present themselves every day but they go unnoticed. These events are in our view but we are blind to their impact.

Soon, we will hopefully find out what actually took place that tragic day more than 60 years ago. Perhaps there are other individuals out there, like me, who will finally have the opportunity or the courage to release what they know without fear of DOJ or governmental reprisals. Perhaps someone involved will actually confess to what they did.

Let's just be honest as to what took place: A coup d'etat of the most powerful man in the world. With that full disclosure and transparency, perhaps the great wound America has lived with since Nov. 22, 1963, can heal.

These final questions remain:

Will knowing what took place as to the Kennedy Assassination enable us to address those unelected officials, call them the Deep State or whatever label you choose, who are still operating with unlimited power in America?

Are unelected individuals or entities that have the power to take unlimited action not to be held accountable?

Can we learn from our past mistakes and correct our direction?

Will history repeat itself as the Deep State and the absolute power of the military industrial complex continue to shape our great country's future to fight endless wars?

Sadly, we continue to see evidence of that every day.

Hidden in plain sight.

– Attorney Kevin F. Jursinski

Photos

The names and photos highlighted here do not include everyone or everything, but they offer added context to the stories I've shared.

First and foremost, I wanted to honor my family. And I wanted to pay tribute to the American Soldiers that I've known. Their sacrifices have never been forgotten. We enjoy the freedoms offered in America due to these fearless warriors.

Also included are pictures of Joseph Helmich and his *KAK: Manuscript*, which I've kept secure for decades. I wanted to share what my client experienced as an American Soldier who believed he was serving his country and did his best to honor that pledge.

There are a series of photos that mark the many events involving the outstanding individuals I have met and lessons I have learned from my involvement in sports. These experiences led up to my time as an NFL agent, including my role in the sale of the original iconic Heisman Trophy. The great memories and friends that I made along the way show that sports are a large part of the fabric of our American Society and are a great training ground for our warrior class.

Finally, I've included charts that illustrate how the Viet Nam Draft Lottery was conducted. It was surreal to have your fate decided by a random set of numbers. And those results had dire consequences for so many young brave Americans who might not have anticipated being in a combat setting other than by conscription.

Family Matters

My brother, Ken "Kenny" Jursinski, was a brave American Soldier. Above he is shown with his platoon members at the "Hanoi Hilton." In 1968, Kenny was stationed at Camp Radcliff outside of An Khe in the Central Highlands of Viet Nam.

My mom, Natalie "Tillie" Jursinski, posing with me Christmas 1998. She was a strong and determined woman who taught me so much through her words and actions, but her love of family remains the biggest impact on my life. While I was prepared to serve my country, it was the tenacity of my mom that shielded me from war and provided me a new path to reshape my life.

Family Matters

I'm forever proud of my dad for all he did for me, but I also admire his courage during World War II. Captain Frank "Jay" Jursinski served in the U.S. Army's 158th Engineer's Battalion. He led his company during the Battle of the Bulge from Dec. 1944 until Jan. 1945. The 158th provided defense in areas around Bastogne, Belgium. My father also assisted the residents of Laroche, Belgium by providing them supplies. My dad was a combat-wounded, decorated Veteran.

Captain Frank "Jay" Jursinski after his Jeep was hit by German artillery in the Ardennes Forest outside of Bastogne, Belgium. Notwithstanding being wounded, Capt. Jursinski still led his company during the Battle of the Bulge, considered the bloodiest battle of World War II.

My wife's uncle, Army Sergeant Bernard Deem was a member of the 193rd Glider Infantry Regiment, an airborne infantry regiment during World War II and part of the 17th Airborne Division that fought during the Battle of the Bulge. While they did not know each other, my dad and Sergeant Deem fought bravely in this same epic battle. Unfortunately, Sergeant Deem was killed in action in that battle.

The Heroic American Soldiers

Lance Corporal Raymond Hodorowski, United States Marine Corps. Ray was one of the toughest guys from my hometown. I could not believe that this badass was killed. Ray was from South Lorain, Ohio. He died in Quang Tri, South Viet Nam. He was only 21 years old (8/29/45 to 3/6/67).

Private First Class Robert J. Nagy, United States Army. Bob was a great friend from our neighborhood and lifelong friend of my brother. He's the reason Ken volunteered for deployment to Viet Nam so he could serve with him. Bob was from Lorain, Ohio. He died in Bing Long, Viet Nam. He was only 20 years old (4/7/47 to 10/17/67).

The Heroic American Soldiers

Private First Class Ronald Ralich, United States Marine Corps. Ron was another fallen soldier from my neighborhood. My brother dated his sister for quite some time. Ron was from Lorain, Ohio. He died in Thua Thien, South Viet Nam. He was only 19 years old (9/19/46 to 5/29/66).

Captain Donald R. Bonko, United States Military Academy. Don attended my high school, Lorain St. Mary High School and was an All-Ohio fullback. He died in Viet Nam. He was only 28 years old (12/16/36 to 11/26/65).

<u>Interview With A Spy: Joseph Helmich</u>

This is how I remember Joseph Helmich from my interview with him in 1982 at the federal prison in Talladega, Alabama. This image is from an interview with CBS News Nightwatch with Charlie Rose that he gave after his conviction.

Joseph Helmich is shown here answering questions from the media outside the courthouse during his trial in 1981. He never took the stand to tell his side of the story on the record.

Interview With A Spy: Joseph Helmich

This is the first of four notebooks that comprise the *KAK: Manuscript.* In Russian, KAK means "How." Joseph Helmich wrote the manuscript while in prison and before we met for our interview.

My Mercedes-Benz, leather-bound owner's manual cover, where I placed the manuscript once I left Talladega prison. The notebooks fit perfectly. They remain tucked inside this manual cover.

<u>Interview With A Spy: Joseph Helmich</u>

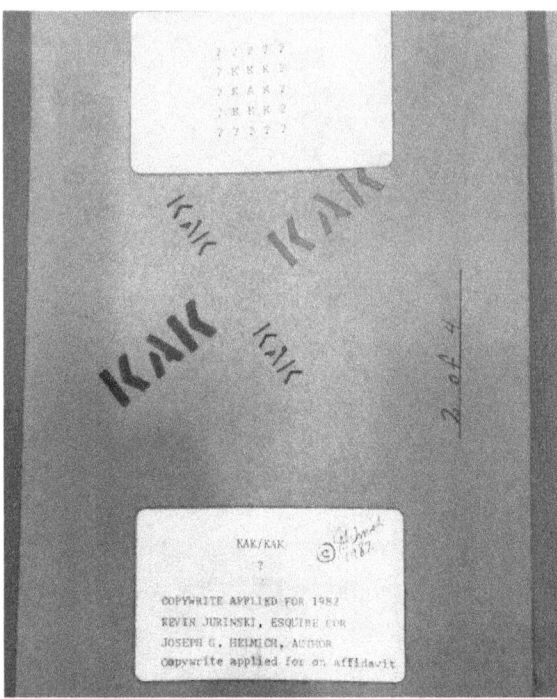

This is the second of the four notebooks, and it is exactly how Helmich prepared it before I ever met him. When he handed me the notebooks, my name was already typed on a label and stuck to the cover.

These four notebooks make up the complete *KAK: Manuscript*. I've kept them safe and secure since the moment Helmich entrusted me with telling his story.

Interview With A Spy: Joseph Helmich

U.S. Department of Justice

RECEIVED APR 0 4 2025

Washington, D.C. 20530

March 28, 2025

Dear Sir/Madam:

This is in response to your request for records, Tracking Number, ▮▮▮▮▮▮▮▮ Your Freedom of Information Act and/or Privacy Act (FOIA/PA) request was received by this office which serves as the receipt and referral unit for FOIA/PA requests addressed to the Department of Justice (DOJ). Federal agencies are required to respond to a FOIA request within 20 business days. This period does not begin until the request is actually received by the component within the DOJ that maintains the records sought, or ten business days after the request is received in this office, whichever is earlier.

We have referred your request to the DOJ component(s) you have designated or, based on descriptive information you have provided, to the component(s) most likely to have the records. All future inquiries concerning the status of your request should be addressed to the office(s) listed below:

FOIA/PA
Executive Office for U.S. Attorneys
Department of Justice
Suite 5.400
175 N. Street N.E.
Washington, DC 20530-0001
(202) 252-6020

Sincerely,

MRUFOIA
Logistics Management
Facilities and Administrative Services Staff
Justice Management Division

This is one of many Freedom of Information Act requests I made surrounding Joseph Helmich-related records and I'm still waiting for an official response other than these generic replies. I needed to hire a private investigator to find the trial transcript.

Glory Days

When I attended the University of Akron and played varsity football, eight other players from Lorain County joined me. They included, front row, left to right: Bernie Wolak, Billy Lemley, co-captain Nate Hagins and Dennis Jones. Back row, standing, left to right: Lynn Livelsberger, me, Jack Beidler, Wayne Harrison and Dave Leininger.

Our fraternity gathered for our annual photo at an old-time strip club in downtown Canton, Ohio perhaps reflective of the priority that some of us had. I am directly under the "Liberal Discounters" sign in the middle of the photo.

Glory Days

Our security company assignments took us to some amazing events. We did backstage and stadium security for the Crosby, Stills, Nash and Young concert at then-Rich Stadium in Buffalo, New York, on Aug. 11, 1974. They played to a crowd of 100,000-plus. We maintained order at this event and others, such as the Rolling Stones concert at Cleveland Stadium in 1975 where I worked backstage security.

This is a certificate given to me by my construction crew on our flight back to the states on my 19th birthday. It is a map of the trek we made when working in Alaska the summer before my sophomore year in college. Our base camp was on the northernmost part of Alaska, Prudhoe Bay, directly on the Arctic Ocean, more than 5,000 miles from the sunny beaches of Southwest Florida.

Glory Days

In 2010, the Lorain Sports Hall of Fame inducted our 1966 Lorain St. Mary football team. I was a junior on the 1966 team that went 9-0 (I am in the top row, sixth player from the left). While we outscored our foes 279-86, four of our victories were by eight points or less. Despite having just under 300 students in the school, United Press ranked us No. 8 in its state poll.

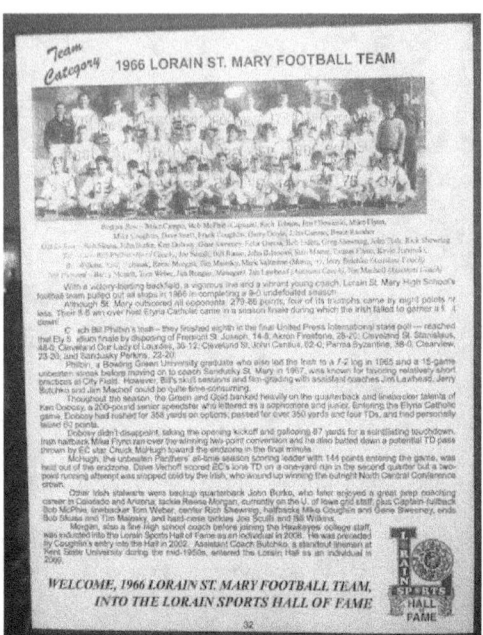

After going 9-0 in 1966, Lorain St. Mary went 9-0 again in 1967 winning our second conference championship in a row, setting the all-time Lorain County (Ohio) win streak record at 25 straight games that still stands. Tim Rose was voted Northeast Ohio Coach of the Year in his first head coaching job and our team was ranked No. 5 in the State of Ohio (Class A). That 1967 team was inducted into the Lorain County Sports Hall of Fame in 2005 and three of us on that team received full-ride football scholarships to major universities.

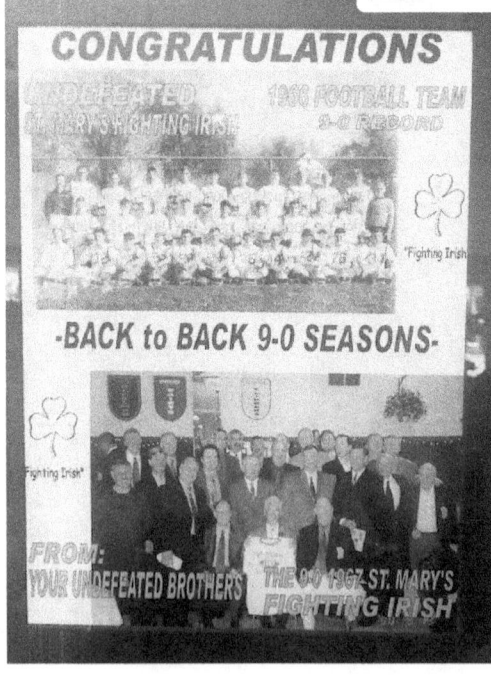

<u>Glory Days</u>

In 1983, Darlene's hometown of Springfield, Ohio was featured inside the 50th Anniversary Issue of *Newsweek*.

FIFTIETH ANNIVERSARY

when one of the Bushnells of High Street was taken to court by his mistress, he had to leave town, and the children of the better families were forbidden to read the stories in the papers; it was too awful. In the new era, even casual sex had become a fact of life, celebrated in rock songs, anatomized on X-rated film and practiced with increasing openness. Caro Bayley scandalized her family in the '40s merely by announcing her intent to go out drinking beer with the boys. When her daughter Caro-Gray went on noonday spins with her North High girl-friends 30 years later with a ration of joints, a jug of screwdrivers and Elton John or Joni Mitchell on the car radio, she didn't find it necessary to confess; in her generation, to get high was no longer a sin but a trip.

Valerie Weber did not surrender to the

My wife Darlene is joined by five other cheerleaders for *Newsweek's* 50th Anniversary Issue while she attended North High School. From front to back: Sue Schultz, Marty Flood, Valerie Weber, Pam Crummy, Darlene and Patti Allen.

The Heisman Trophy

A photo of the original Heisman Trophy sculpture created by Frank Eliscu on the countertop in my client's kitchen. All the trophies given out each year are made from a cast of this original statue. Very few people in the world ever have seen or held the original Heisman statue. It was amazing to see this in person before I helped auction it off on behalf of the family in 2005 for $240,000.

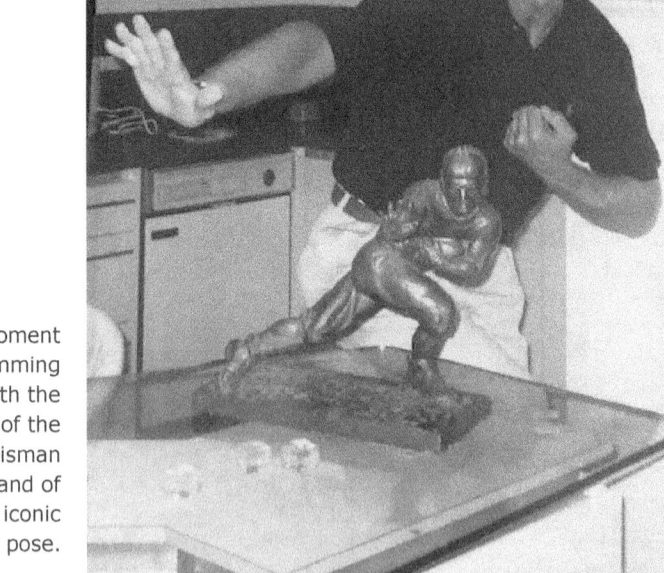

Proud moment for me hamming it up with the sculpture of the original Heisman Trophy and of course the iconic Heisman pose.

The Heisman Trophy

Me and Darlene posing with the Heisman Trophy at Sotheby's in New York City, Dec. 9, 2005, before the trophy was presented for auction.

The Heisman Trophy

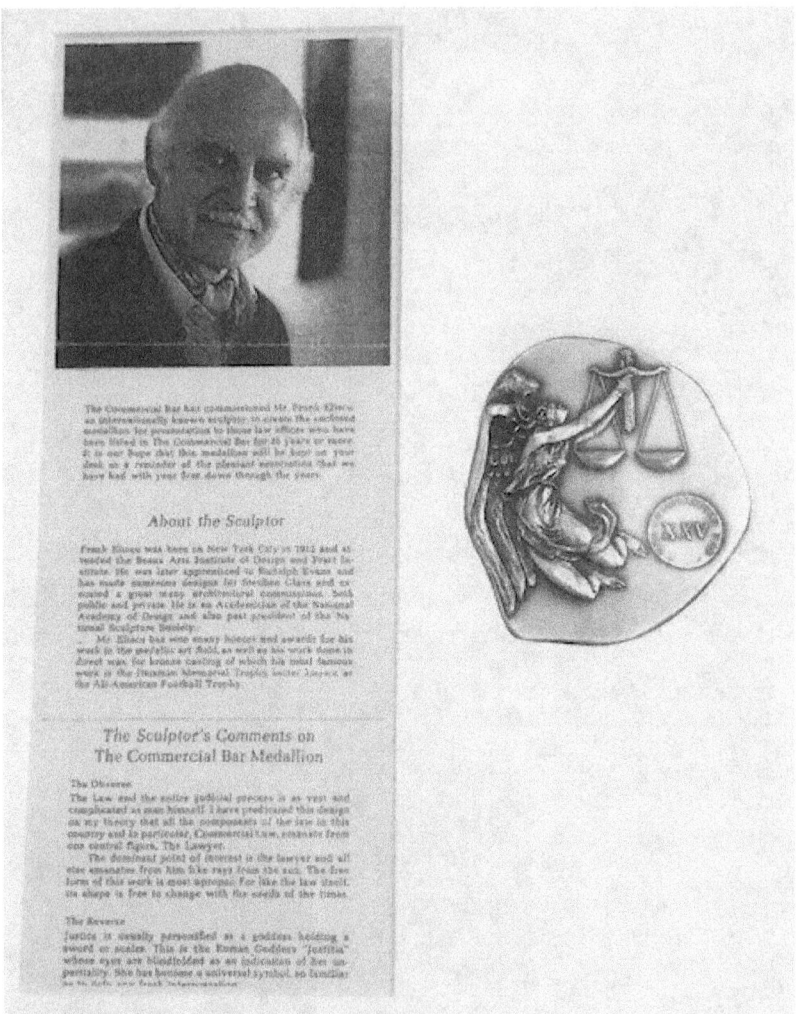

The Eliscu family gave me an original Frank Eliscu statue, *Daniel in the Lion's Den*. They also gave me an original silver medallion, above right in image, created by Mr. Eliscu for the Commercial Litigation society and it is a treasured memento.

Sports Agent

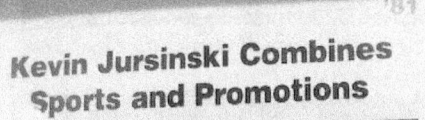

Kevin Jursinski Combines Sports and Promotions

Florida sports agent Kevin Jursinski (JD) is proud of his growing business he has built over the past six years.

Jursinski is the executive vice-president of KC Management, a sports and entertainment management company. His wife, Darlene, is president of the company.

They represent athletes in the National Football League, Canadian Football League and professional baseball. Other clients include actresses and actors, business professionals, published authors and professional coaches.

Some of their clients include: Mike Bartrum, New England Patriots; Alundis Brice, Dallas Cowboys; Chad Epperson, Boston Red Sox; Melvin Johnson, Tampa Bay Buccaneers; Tony Stargell, Kansas City Chiefs; General James L. Dozier, author; and

former team captains or quarterbacks."

"We stick with the players once they sign with us. They become a part of the KC Management family," he said. "We take

Darlene and I dabbled in the sports agency business for a number of years: KC Management. We represented some great clients, including Dexter McCleon, cornerback for the Super Bowl Champion St. Louis Rams; Mike Bartrum, long snapper for the Super Bowl Patriots and Eagles; Alundis Brice, cornerback for the Super Bowl Champion Dallas Cowboys; and tailback Earnest Graham of the Tampa Bay Buccaneers.

Sports Agent

Pictured left to right: Dexter McCleon, starting cornerback for the Super Bowl Champion St. Louis Rams, me, his mother Beverly McCleon, friend Ron Johnson and sister Tamara McCleon. Photo was taken in the family area outside the locker room at the then-Trans World Dome in St. Louis. I negotiated a $20 million contract for Dexter with the Rams, then later negotiated a $14.3 million contract for Dexter with the Kansas City Chiefs.

This is me with Olympians Carl Lewis and Leroy Burrell (far right), both Olympic gold medalists in Miami after the Hurricanes and Houston played their season opener at the Orange Bowl in 1991. Lewis and Burrell held the title of the fastest man in the world at different times. I negotiated an appearance contract for Lewis with the City of Fort Myers. Also pictured is a former Hurricanes' player, a sports management company consultant, NFL coach Dan Daniel and in front, one of my partners in KC Management, Chico Rivera.

The Viet Nam Draft Lottery

Table	Date of Drawing	Applied to Year of Birth	APN
1970	December 1, 1969	1944-1950	195
1971	July 1, 1970	1951	125
1972	August 5, 1971	1952	95
1973	February 2, 1972	1953	95
1974	March 8, 1973	1954	95
1975	March 20, 1974	1955	95
1976	March 12, 1975	1956	95

The table above shows a breakdown of the Viet Nam Draft Lottery formula by year, date of drawing and year of birth for each eligible American. I was drafted in the very first draft occurring Dec. 1, 1969. *Image courtesy of the Selective Service System website.*

Alphabetical Sequence Chart

1	J
2	G
3	D
4	X
5	N
6	O
7	Z
8	T
9	W
10	P
11	Q
12	Y
13	U
14	C
15	F
16	I
17	K
18	H
19	S
20	L
21	M
22	A
23	R
24	E
25	B
26	V

This table shows a breakdown of how letters were assigned for each draft number in preparation for the Viet Nam Draft Lottery. With the first letter of your last name, your middle initial and your first name being your call sign and number designating the date of birth for selection, I was officially 'JFK 160" for the 1969 draft, the very first military draft in over 25 years in the United States. *Image courtesy of the Selective Service System website.*

The Viet Nam Draft Lottery

SELECTIVE SERVICE SYSTEM
1970 RANDOM SELECTION SEQUENCE, BY MONTH AND DAY

	Jan	Feb	Mar	Apr	May	Jun	Jul	Aug	Sep	Oct	Nov	Dec
1	305	086	108	032	330	249	093	111	225	359	019	129
2	159	144	029	271	298	228	350	045	161	125	034	328
3	251	297	267	083	040	301	115	261	049	244	348	157
4	215	210	275	081	276	020	279	145	232	202	266	165
5	101	214	293	269	364	028	188	054	082	024	310	056
6	224	347	139	253	155	110	327	114	006	087	076	010
7	306	091	122	147	035	085	050	168	008	234	051	012
8	199	181	213	312	321	366	013	048	184	283	097	105
9	194	338	317	219	197	335	277	106	263	342	080	043
10	325	216	323	218	065	206	284	021	071	220	282	041
11	329	150	136	014	037	134	248	324	158	237	046	039
12	221	068	300	346	133	272	015	142	242	072	066	314
13	318	152	259	124	295	069	042	307	175	138	126	163
14	238	004	354	231	178	356	331	198	001	294	127	026
15	017	089	169	273	130	180	322	102	113	171	131	320
16	121	212	166	148	055	274	120	044	207	254	107	096
17	235	189	033	260	112	073	098	154	255	288	143	304
18	140	292	332	090	278	341	190	141	246	005	146	128
19	058	025	200	336	075	104	227	311	177	241	203	240
20	280	302	239	345	183	360	187	344	063	192	185	135
21	186	363	334	062	250	060	027	291	204	243	156	070
22	337	290	265	316	326	247	153	339	160	117	009	053
23	118	057	256	252	319	109	172	116	119	201	182	162
24	059	236	258	002	031	358	023	036	195	196	230	095
25	052	179	343	351	361	137	067	286	149	176	132	084
26	092	365	170	340	357	022	303	245	018	007	309	173
27	355	205	268	074	296	064	289	352	233	264	047	078
28	077	299	223	262	308	222	088	167	257	094	281	123
29	349	285	362	191	226	353	270	061	151	229	099	016
30	164	----	217	208	103	209	287	333	315	038	174	003
31	211	----	030	----	313	----	193	011	----	079	----	100

This table shows a breakdown of the Viet Nam Draft Lottery and the position by day and month of your draft number. I was born Sept. 22, 1950 and with the Alphabetical Sequence applied designating my draft call name, I was "JFK 160" for the 1969 draft in which the first 195 numbers were called to service. *Image courtesy of the Selective Service System website.*

Acknowledgments

First and foremost, I want to thank my wife Darlene, who has been with me through most of my adult life, for supporting me on this long journey to bring this book to life.

The day I met Darlene was unquestionably the best day of my life. She is my true love, my best friend and the inspiration of my life. She has always been there for me in the good times and bad. Darlene helped me address my life goals at a time when I had lost my way.

My three daughters Jamie, Lauren and Kara are amazing women who were guided in their lives by their mother. I am so very proud of our daughters for the wonderful person that each one of them has become. They are all successful in their careers and also are loving mothers to their children.

I want to thank my parents, who were wonderful role models for me. Even though at times I did not always live up to what they knew I should be, I know that they are proud of the man that I ultimately did become.

I want to thank my brother Ken, who like our father, was an American Soldier, for his bravery. Ken sacrificed for this country and served honorably in the U.S. Army. His heroic service and decision to volunteer to fight in Viet Nam was an inspiration to me in writing this book.

I want to thank my wonderful grandparents for their support. My grandmother Stephanie Jurczynski was the ultimate loving grandmother who never hesitated to sacrifice for her grandsons while always having a kind word to say. My grandfather Mike was the strong, silent, hard-working type. I called him "Iron Mike" since even on the day he died he had a grip that could crush your hand. My grandmother Pauline ("Baba") Carson was one resilient lady and I learned some life lessons from observing her.

I want to thank my aunt, Sr. Mary Patricia (Stephanie) Jurczynska (our family's last name had many spellings), for her guidance. She was a dedicated Catholic and devoted her entire life to Christ as a nun and educator. She was an extremely intelligent individual, finishing her career as a principal at a Catholic school in our hometown. She was well educated, obtaining a PhD in education.

She wrote her dissertation for her master's degree on the contributions of Poland to the American Civil War: "A Study of the Participation of the Poles in the American Civil War." This work complemented the more widely known contributions of Poland to the American Revolutionary War effort.

Her paper identified numerous Polish officers fighting for the Union Army and their military battles. It should be noted that the first military officer killed in the American Civil War was Union battalion commander Captain Constantin Blandowski. A Catholic nun writing on U.S. Military history and battles, Sister Patricia's paper was so well received it has been identified as an important historical work and can be located in libraries including St. John's College Library in Cleveland.

Amazingly, Sr. Patricia also produced a religious TV show on a Cleveland TV station in the 1970s. She was one of the first female producers of a TV show in Cleveland and I believe the first nun to produce a TV show.

She was very accomplished. I had the privilege to give the eulogy at her funeral. I was so very proud of the life she lived devoted to Christ while at the same time giving so much to our society from her dedicated and selfless service to education and her writings.

Personally, what I remember Sister Patricia for over all of her accomplishments is the amount of prayers she always said for me. She constantly prayed for me and sent me cards and thoughts with dedication of Masses and prayers. I can't begin to count the number of times in my life that I was in some tough situations and generally went unscathed. I truly believe that was because of all the prayers she said for me. My guardian angel had to be on his toes with all the prayers from my aunt that asked God to watch over me. To paraphrase Morgan Wallen: I hope Sister Patricia knows that all those prayers she said for me finally made their way on through. I love you Sister Pat.

I want to thank Jean Helmich for her steadfast support on this project. Once she approved this book, she never wavered in encouraging me to tell Joe's story. She believed that I would get this project done to bring clarity to the charges against her husband in hopes of setting the record straight. And ultimately, finally publish Joe's full manuscript so a jury of his peers could hear his side of the story - in his own words - and determine for themselves his innocence or guilt.

I want to extend a special thank you to Joe Helmich, who had confidence in me from our very first meeting and entrusted me to bring his story to life. I was not able to do that while he was alive, but I never gave up and honored my promise to him. Rest in Peace, Joe. I will see you on the other side.

I want to thank my editors, Dave Kratzke and Craig Handel, for all of their hard work and input in helping me create a polished product to publish. They also supported me through this effort and provided keen insight.

I also appreciate the input from my friend Ron Curry and his wife Lorrie Curry for their input. They are the parents of a current Secret Service agent and Ron was himself a Secret Service agent who held a spot on the Presidential detail for Ronald Reagan. They both provided comments and perspective into this project.

I also want to thank a friend and client, Kenneth Shemenski, U.S. Army officer, Viet Nam Veteran and Green Beret, for his insights and thoughts on the Viet Nam War.

I want to thank Ron Deem for his input and perspective on this book. Ron has been one of my best friends for more than 50 years as well as my college roommate and teammate on two of our Kent State flag football championship teams. Until I interviewed him for this book, Ron never really told me much about the shootings on May 4. Perhaps too painful. Upon questioning, Ron provided personal insight on the Kent shootings on May 4, having been on the Kent State Commons and luckily surviving the indiscriminate shooting by members of the Ohio National Guard. I hope this book soothes some of his pain.

I appreciate my other friends for their support and encouragement to me to write this book. I especially want to thank my friends Dominick Ferrante and Amy Ferrante for their support. Dominick is a former combat tested Marine and experienced law enforcement officer who shared his thoughts with me on this project. Dominick and his lovely wife Amy are also great role models since their own son, Charlie Ferrante, is a cadet attending West Point. Charlie Ferrante is himself an American Soldier like his father. Charlie has joined the Young Warrior Class in America. I also want to thank Amy, who did an outstanding job on the artwork for the front and back book cover and added some great ideas for the back cover. Thank you Amy!

I want to thank Don Corbett for his tireless detective work in unearthing the elusive trial transcript from Joseph Helmich's case. His efforts helped bring the full scope of the trial into focus and confirmed much of my suspicions about how the case was prosecuted against Helmich.

I want to thank and dedicate this book to all the brave American Soldiers, both men and women, who answer the call each and every day to defend our freedom around the globe.

They are True Warriors.

To all of those men and women who have given the ultimate sacrifice and especially those Viet Nam Veterans who may not have received the proper respect and appreciation from America for their service in Viet Nam, I want to personally thank each and every one of them for allowing me and my family to live under the Flag of Freedom in America.

It is fitting to quote from the Memorial page of the late Marine Ronnie Ralich: "Please watch over America, it still needs your strength, courage and faithfulness, especially now. Rest in peace with the angels," Lucy Micik. And as posted by Ronnie's fellow Viet Nam Veterans of the Second Battalion, First Marines: "Take your warrior's rest for a duty well done. Semper Fi, Marine!"

In closing, the quote from Lance Corporal Raymond Hodorowski's Memorial page sums up my feelings in writing this book: "The war may be forgotten but the Warrior will always be remembered!!!! All gave some, some gave All. Rest in peace Raymond," Jerry Sandwisch, Viet Nam Veteran.

About The Author

For over 40 years, Kevin F. Jursinski has served Southwest Florida clients in the areas of real estate, business litigation and construction law. He is recognized as one of the premier attorneys in Florida and also has a specialized practice in the area of gaming law in regard to game promotions, arcade centers and video games.

Mr. Jursinski is rated AV Preeminent®, which is the highest-ranking level of professional excellence, skill and integrity under the Martindale-Hubbell® Peer Review Ratings™ system and has maintained that distinction for the past 20 years. He has an exceptional overall Martindale-Hubbell Peer Review Rating of 4.9 on a 5.0 scale.

He also has earned a perfect 10.0 score on AVVO.com, a lawyer rating and referral website. He has been recognized by "The Best Lawyers in America," a significant honor within the legal profession, placing him in the top 5% of all attorneys in America.

Since 2010, he has been named a Florida Super Lawyer by Super Lawyers Magazine.

In addition, Mr. Jursinski is one of the nine triple Florida Bar Board Certified out of more than 100,000 in the state and is the only attorney in Florida who is triple-Florida Bar Board Certified in the areas of real estate law, construction law and business litigation.

Mr. Jursinski's expertise extends to being admitted to practice in all Florida state courts and the U.S. District Court for the Middle District of Florida. He is a certified circuit court mediator as well as a state-qualified arbitrator. He also serves as an expert witness in real estate-related cases.

A graduate of Kent State University (B.A. Social Theory/Criminal Justice), Mr. Jursinski graduated in the top 15 percent of his class at Ohio Northern University Pettit College of Law (J.D. 1980) while completing his three-year degree in just two years.

The Law Office of Jursinski and Murphy is located in Fort Myers, Florida. It is a family-run business. Wife Darlene is the office manager.

Daughter and Attorney Kara Jursinski Murphy is a partner of the law firm, is also AV-rated and is a Florida Bar Board Certified real estate attorney, focusing on both litigation and transactional law.

Daughter Jamie Lampitt is the Manager of Title Masters title insurance agency, another family-owned business of the Jursinski family. Daughter Lauren Smith is Kevin's paralegal. Son-in-law and Attorney William Murphy is also a key member of the law firm and focuses his practice in the area of construction law.

When he's not working or writing, Kevin competes in a variety of sports. He and his wife Darlene also enjoy watching their eight grandchildren take part in athletics and other school events.

Kevin is an avid Cleveland Browns fan and has been for more than 60 years. He is one of the few people on the planet that can claim that they attended the last Cleveland Browns NFL title game, the 1964 national championship game in Cleveland, and also attended the last AFC championship game the Browns played, the 1990 AFC championship game versus the Denver Broncos held in Denver's Mile High Stadium. Kevin has attended a number of Super Bowls in his life and is hoping to attend one in which the Browns are playing for the Super Bowl title.

Thank You

Thank you for reading *Interview With A Spy*. It has been a pleasure to share my experiences with you, to honor the American Soldier and to finally deliver on my promise to my client to tell his story. If you enjoyed this book, please consider leaving a review on the website where you bought the book.

ALSO FROM BIG KAT KREATIVE

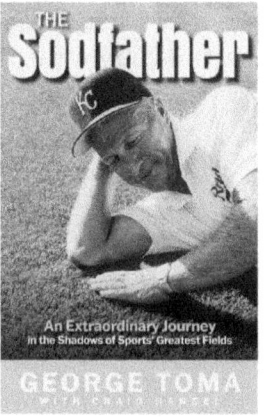

AVAILABLE WHEREVER BOOKS ARE SOLD

bigkatkreative.com

www.ingramcontent.com/pod-product-compliance
Lightning Source LLC
Chambersburg PA
CBHW070912120626
46546CB00001B/238